BIBLE
KEYWORDING
GUIDE

BEYOND THE HIGHLIGHTER

beyondthehighlighter.com

Copyright © 2022 by Rob Sinclair (Beyond the Highlighter)

IT IS ILLEGAL AND UNETHICAL TO DUPLICATE COPYRIGHTED MATERIAL.

All rights reserved. No part of this publication may be reproduced, stored in a retrieval system or transmitted in any form or by any means - electronic, mechanical, photo- copy, recording, or any other – except for brief quotations in printed reviews, without the prior permission of the publisher.

Bible Keywording Guide logo mark designed by Evangela Creative
Cover design by Chad Landman
Edited by Dawn Weaver – *maidtoedit.com*

Published by Kaio Publications, Inc.
www.kaiopublications.org

Scripture quotations taken from the New American Standard Bible® (NASB),
Copyright © 1960, 1962, 1963, 1968, 1971, 1972, 1973,
1975, 1977, 1995 by The Lockman Foundation
Used by permission. www.lockman.org

ISBN-13: 978-1-952955-31-0

Printed in the United States of America

ACKNOWLEDGMENTS

It is said that we all stand on the shoulders of those who came before us. That is certainly true for the inspiration behind this project. A big thanks to:

Denny Petrillo and Michael Hite, for sparking the passion and inspiration behind these guides.

Dawn Weaver and Chad Landman, for keeping the dream alive.

Joe and Erin Wells, for stopping by the booth and changing the game.

My beautiful bride, Kylie Sinclair, for marking her Bible the same way I do.

CONTENTS

INTRODUCTION 5
1 PETER 12
  STUDYING 1 PETER 13
  GENERAL INFORMATION 14
  KEY CONCEPTS 15
  KEY WORDS 20
    SUFFERING 21
    DO 25
    GOOD 27
    EVIL 31
    GLORY 33
    FAITH 37
    HOLY 41
    LIVE 45
    GRACE 51
    BEHAVIOR 53
    SUBMIT 57
    REVEALED 61
  OPTIONAL WORDS 63
  KEY CONCLUSIONS 65
  MY KEY WORDS 66

2 PETER 68
STUDYING 2 PETER 69
GENERAL INFORMATION 70
KEY CONCEPTS 71
KEY WORDS 78
KNOWLEDGE 79
DESTRUCTION 83
DAY 87
RIGHTEOUS 91
WORD 95
JUDGMENT 99
GODLINESS 101
WAY 105
PROMISE 107
OPTIONAL WORDS 109
KEY CONCLUSIONS 110
MY KEY WORDS 111

BIBLE KEYWORDING GUIDE
Beyond the Highlighter

1 & 2 PETER

ROB SINCLAIR

INTRODUCTION

BEYOND THE HIGHLIGHTER

As a preacher, I am regularly asked, "I have read the Bible cover to cover several times; what do I do next?" Maybe you have asked something similar regarding your own Bible study and have felt disengaged from God's Word. My answer is to study a Bible book more in depth than you've ever thought possible...and make it look easy with the *Bible Keywording Guide*.

The *Bible Keywording Guide* (BKG) is an easy-to-use series of manuals designed to help Bible students of any level identify and mark critical information found in each book of the Bible. This includes things like: key words, purpose statements, prayers, etc. Each Bible book has its own set of peculiarities that, when marked, help the reader understand what the author is really saying.

I was told once by a friend that before he understood what keywording was, a mechanical pencil and a yellow highlighter were "standard procedure" when it came to marking important ideas and insights in his Bible. Maybe this sentiment has been true for you as well. Engage in this process and see how the *Bible Keywording Guide* will take you beyond the highlighter and bring you to a whole new level of Bible study!

THE IMPORTANCE OF KEYWORDING

WHAT IS A KEY WORD? – A key word is a word that holds a significant theological meaning and is often repeated by the author to convey his points and purposes for writing. Key words are related to the themes and overall scope of the books. Without them, the author's emphasis and meanings would be greatly diminished, and even nonexistent in many cases. Keywording is an essential component of Bible study (i.e. exegesis) and is done using colors and/or symbols to distinguish certain words in the text. Leave the highlighter in the drawer...you're using a dynamic and multicolored system now!

FREQUENCY – Some key words are used a lot; others are used less frequently. If a writer uses a word consistently – repeating it over and over – then that word is a key word. Sometimes, however, key words are used less frequently and may not be as noticeable, purely based on quantity. Words like *of* and *the* would not be considered key words, even though they are some of the most frequently used words in the Bible. On the other hand, some words are extremely theologically charged, but aren't used much. For example, *wisdom* (*sophia*) is a very important and theologically significant word in the book of James, but it is only used five times in the letter.

WORD FAMILIES – Word families are filtered in the BKG to make keywording even easier. Root words and lemmas will be distinguished in this guide with an *R* or *L*. A root word (*R*) is a word that encompasses an entire family of words joined together by the same stem, whereas a lemma (*L*) is a specific word within that root's family. This distinction is made in the BKG due to the fact that sometimes an entire family of words helps the reader understand how the writer is developing a particular concept. On the other hand, sometimes only a particular word within that larger word family is theologically significant. An excellent example to distinguish the importance of these elements would be the root word, *kaleō*, which means "to call" or "to invite." Words like *parakaleō* (comfort/urge), *paraklēsis* (exhort), and *ekklēsia* (church/assembly) are all lemma forms of the root word *kaleō*. If the key word to be marked is *ekklēsia*, then there is no need to mark all forms of its root word, *kaleō*.

CHAPTER-SPECIFIC KEY WORDS – Most key words in a Bible book are used throughout the entire work, but some only make a strong appearance in a chapter or two. Consider *wisdom* (*sophia*) again. Of its 28 uses in 1 Corinthians, *wisdom* appears 26 times in the first three chapters. The idea may be present in other parts of the book, but the word itself doesn't make much of an appearance elsewhere. Just because a word makes a strong showing for a few chapters, and then very little afterwards, does not mean it isn't a key word. Chapter-specific key words must still be considered because of their theological contributions to their books.

OPTIONAL WORDS – Most of these guides will contain an "Optional Words" list. Optional Words will be those words that are of some interest, but may not be used for a few different reasons: (1) they may not be exceedingly theologically significant, (2) they may be used so frequently that to mark them would mean making your Bible pages extremely crowded or too busy to focus on the other words marked, or (3) they may just be synonyms to the key words. It will be at the user's discretion whether or not to mark these words. In cases where references for these words are not provided, a Biblical concordance will help you identify their uses if you choose to mark them.

KEY CONCEPTS

The BKG will also assist you in the identification and marking of other important exegetical/Bible study elements when available. For instance, the New Testament epistles will contain things like purpose statements, prayers, and petition verbs. (Don't worry; we'll get into that later!) Many books in the Old Testament will have important textual markers and key phrases that should be marked to better understand the thought and flow of the book. With these guides, you won't miss a thing!

When available, dates of books, authors, genres, places of writing, recipients of the book, occasion of the book, etc. will be included to assist you in the study process. These elements help to form the context of each book and should be generally understood as you begin marking your Bible.

WHY YOU SHOULD KEYWORD YOUR BIBLE

SIMPLICITY – The BKG will give you a comprehensive list of all the key words in each book you're studying. You won't have to waste any time trying to determine which words and concepts you should be focusing on.

EMPHASIS ON ORIGINAL LANGUAGES – Not only will you have a complete list of key words, but you will know where those words occur in the *original language*. THIS IS THE HEART AND SOUL OF KEYWORDING! **HERE'S WHY:**

Some key words are translated differently in English while the original language never changes. A good example is the word *faith*. In many New Testament books, *faith* (*pisteuō*) is also translated as "believe," "entrusted," "sure," etc., but it remains the same Greek word. An untrained eye will miss these instances, but the BKG eliminates the possibility of overlooking or missing a key word in literal translations because of its emphasis on the original languages. Why settle for a method that only teaches you to look for certain English words when the BKG streamlines the process in the author's original language?

It's also important to realize that some words in English Bibles are not always identical in meaning. One of the best examples of this would be the word *love* in John 21:15-17. The first two times Jesus asks Peter if he loves Him, Jesus says, "Do you love (*agapaō*) Me?" to which Peter replies, "Yes, Lord; You know that I love (*phileō*) You." If the reader is not careful, he will have missed the fact that the Greek word for *love* changed a few times in this passage, thinking that the same idea for love was present for this entire encounter. The BKG will help identify these types of occurrences so that the true meaning of the text will be revealed.

NOTE: While keywording passages using this guide, you may realize that you will skip over the English word several times without marking it. Don't be alarmed! This simply means that the word, although translated in English, is not the Greek, Hebrew, or Aramaic word you are supposed to mark. Again, if you mark every occurrence of *love* the same way, you will accidentally equate *agapaō* and *phileō*. However, this should not discourage you from marking synonyms in the text if they are indeed synonyms.

FASTER AND EASIER STUDY – Once your Bible is marked, you will immediately notice the important things next time you open it to study. Do you want to study *suffering* in 1 Peter or show someone how James writes about *wisdom*? Just turn there in your marked Bible and you will see these concepts fly off the page! You won't have to spend precious time scanning paragraph after paragraph for specific words or concepts anymore. Plus, you'll notice how all of those verses are related to one another instantly!

YOUR BIBLE WILL BE BEAUTIFUL – There's something incredibly satisfying about looking down at a freshly marked page of the Bible. Not only will it give you an amazing sense of accomplishment, it could very well inspire your friends and family to study God's Word with you! Marked Bibles tend to be eye-catching and often spark interest in others.

CUSTOMIZE: MAKE YOUR MARK

COMPLETE CUSTOMIZATION – One of the many advantages of the BKG is that it allows for complete customization. Suggestions for colors and symbols will be provided throughout the guides, but you can always decide (and design) for yourself which symbol or mark you'd rather use in the "My Mark" sections. If you just hate the color orange, mix it up and develop your own color system! The suggestions given generally follow a certain pattern (i.e. red is usually used for negative things – yellow is generally used for bright things, etc.). If you don't want to mark one of the key words for whatever reason, simply leave the "Marked" box unchecked for future reference.

"MY KEY WORDS" – If you find some words during your study that you believe are key to the text but are not listed in the guide, add them to the "My Key Words" section toward the back. Fill in the information for these words and design your own symbol for them!

DO SOME COLORFUL RESEARCH – Before you begin marking your Bible, do some research and determine which markers, pens, or pencils suit *your* needs and *your* Bible the best. Some Bible pages are too thin to handle certain brands of markers, and the markers bleed through very easily. Even if a brand of markers is marketed as Bible friendly, caution and experimentation should be used prior to commitment. Feel free to use a combination of these writing utensils. I personally enjoy using colored pencils because they never bleed through, rarely fade, are cost effective, and are standardized in color within their brands.

NOTE: Make sure you have a ruler or other straight edge available when marking straight lines. Squiggly lines made by freehand can look messy!

CHOOSE YOUR LITERAL TRANSLATION

THE BKG IS COMPATIBLE WITH LITERAL TRANSLATIONS OF THE BIBLE – Scriptures in the BKG come from the *New American Standard Bible* (NASB), 1995 update. This translation was chosen for these guides because it remains one of the smoothest and yet most literal translations available on today's market. Other recommended translations to accompany this guide would be the *English Standard Version* (ESV), the *New King James Version* (NKJV), the *King James Version* (KJV), or the *Revised Standard Version* (RSV). Even though the English key words will differ in these translations on occasion (e.g. *brethren* vs. *brothers*), it is still very easy to understand which word should be keyworded to the original languages using this guide.

NOTE: Wide margin Bibles are ideal for keywording! With the amount of marking, underlining, list making, etc. it will be more convenient to have some margin space to play with.

NOTE: On extremely rare occasions it will look like a word is missing in some of the Key Word tables, having been replaced with a (●). Don't worry! This simply means that on this uncommon occasion, the translators are telling us that the original word is there, but is very cumbersome to translate and make it make sense in English given the grammar of the rest of the sentence. Mark these instances as well and know that the meaning of the verse hasn't been changed, but the insertion of the word would make the sentence too awkward in English.

PARAPHRASES AND KEYWORDING – Literal translations are essential to effective keywording. In fact, it is not possible to keyword paraphrased versions like *The Message* because they are not based on the original languages. These versions are more concerned with concepts and not the actual words of the original text.

DYNAMIC EQUIVALENCY AND KEYWORDING – It is possible to keyword translations like the *New Living Translation* (NLT) and the *New International Version* (NIV), but it is not recommended. Translations such as these were translated using the Dynamic Equivalency method, which does not highly emphasize the original languages and sacrifices literality for readability. This is seen very clearly in that the NLT and NIV sometimes translate one Greek word upwards of ten different ways in English to help the reader understand the meaning. However, the meaning actually becomes less clear with every additional word—which many times isn't even synonymous—used in place of the original word.

THE USER SHOULD NOTE that keywording the Biblical text is only one part in the study process. It is not the purpose of the BKG to identify *ALL* important elements in a text, but rather to aid in the identification of key words that may go unseen in English translations.

Certain additional facts and elements will be provided when warranted, but will not be exhaustive. Things such as places, expressions of time, lists, comparisons, contrasts, causes and effects, figures of speech, important conjunctions, verbs, pronouns, etc. will be identified at times, but not extensively since they can be identified in English. However, after the text is keyworded, finding most of these other things will be much easier.

"For you have been born again not of seed which is perishable but imperishable, that is, through the living and enduring word of God."

1 Peter 1:23

1 PETER

STUDYING 1 PETER

1. Read the introduction to one of these guides at least once.
2. Read the "General Information" page to orient yourself to Peter's first epistle.
3. Read 1 Peter all the way through several times to familiarize yourself with the text.
4. Follow the directions found under "Key Concepts." This section will have you mark other important things prior to keywording the book.
5. Keyword the book:
    a. Turn to the first keywording page (e.g. *Suffering*) and locate the suggested symbol for that particular word.
    b. Use the reference list provided in order to locate the English words in your Bible that correspond to their respective Greek word.
    c. Mark the located word with the suggested symbol. Do this for all the key words provided in each guide.
    d. When applicable, answer the questions and/or follow the study prompts included for the words.
    e. For an even deeper study of the word, define it using a reputable Bible dictionary.
6. Mark the Optional Words at your own discretion using the suggested symbols or by creating your own.
7. Complete the "Key Conclusions" section.
8. Utilize the "My Key Words" section when applicable.

GENERAL INFORMATION

AUTHOR PETER THE APOSTLE
Silvanus (Silas) likely served as Peter's scribe and wrote the letter while Peter spoke (cf. 5:12)

GENRE GENERAL EPISTLE

DATE c. 66 A.D.

WRITTEN FR. ROME
Metaphorically compared to "Babylon" (cf. 5:13)

RECIPIENTS TO THOSE WHO RESIDE AS ALIENS, SCATTERED THROUGHOUT PONTUS, GALATIA, CAPPADOCIA, ASIA, AND BITHYNIA, WHO ARE CHOSEN (1:1)
Apparent references to both Jews (e.g. 4:3-4) and Gentiles (e.g. 1:14, 18; 2:9-10) indicate that Peter is writing to a broad *Christian* (4:16) audience.

OCCASION Christian persecution had not yet reached its climax of frequent and violent bloodshed by the time Peter wrote, but he certainly indicates that God's people were starting to feel the heat. Christianity and its high moral standards were still young – intimidating to both those who lived for themselves and those who served idols. Peter writes to encourage these Christians to endure their temporary sufferings at the hands of unbelievers – knowing that Jesus is coming and all will be set right in "His eternal glory" (5:10).

KEY CONCEPTS

PETER – A FISHER OF MEN

From a boisterous fisherman who denied the Lord to a peaceable apostle who went to his own cross for faith in Jesus Christ, Peter came full circle in his service to God. In John 21:18-19, Jesus speaks plainly about Peter's eventual death at the hands of men, that even in his death, Peter would bring glory to God. But before that time came, Peter would do his very best to follow Jesus' simple instruction to "Follow Me!" And he did. He followed Jesus' example through countless instances of sufferings and trials that ultimately qualified him to write the letters he did to the people who needed them the most - suffering saints, people on the edge, people in danger of denying Christ just as Peter himself did. A man who learned obedience the hard way, Peter reminds us of some of the most difficult lessons a suffering Christian can learn.

More is known about the life and times of Peter than any of the original twelve apostles. This makes it easier to construct a timeline of the events surrounding him. Like other timelines in this series, only the events that have bearing on Peter writing his letters will be given. (Otherwise, the Gospel accounts alone would turn this chart into a novel!) Notice that Peter does in fact travel quite a bit outside of Judea and very likely travels through the very regions that he writes his letters to.

DATE	VERSE	EVENT
49	Acts 15:1-12 (esp. vs. 7) Galatians 2:9	Peter addresses the Jerusalem Council and is listed as being a "pillar" in the church. This is the last time Peter is seen in the book of Acts.
50 – 53	Acts 16:6-7	It is entirely possible that when Paul and his companions were on their second missionary journey, they were prevented from going into Asia / Bithynia because Peter was already at work there (or was about to be). Note that Bithynia is one of the regions to whom Peter addressed his letters. (cf. 1 Peter 1:1)
50 – 53	Galatians 1:18; 2:7-9, 11, 14	Due to Paul's frequent references to Peter (Cephas) in Galatians, it is probable that Peter had journeyed through Galatia prior to Paul's arrival. Remember that Galatia is also one of the regions to whom Peter addressed his letters. (cf. 1 Peter 1:1)
50 – 53	1 Corinthians 1:12; 3:22; 9:5; 15:5	Paul frequently references Peter (Cephas) in 1 Corinthians as well, making it possible that Peter had also journeyed to Corinth and was known by the Christians there. If Peter had made it to Corinth, it would have been brief and before A.D. 55 when Paul wrote to the Corinthians for the first time.

54 – 66	Acts 18:2	Peter likely makes it to Rome during this time. Nero becomes the next Roman emperor in A.D. 54, which ends Claudius' ban on Jews in the city of Rome and clears the path for Peter.
66	**1 Peter 1:1; 5:12-13**	**PETER WRITES HIS FIRST LETTER WHILE IN ROME**
67	**2 Peter 1:1; 3:1**	**PETER WRITES HIS SECOND LETTER WHILE IN ROME.** He considers his death to be "imminent" (2 Peter 1:14-15).
67	2 Peter 1:14-15; 2 Timothy 4:6-8	Peter is martyred in Rome about the same time as Paul.

Question:

- After reading the verses provided in the timeline above, what is your conclusion about Peter's travels? Do these events seem probable? What are some of your own conclusions about how Peter spread the Gospel abroad?

- Regarding the subject matter of Peter's letters, why is it significant that it's very likely he had visited the Christians he wrote to?

Notes:

PURPOSE STATEMENT

Peter's purpose statement (5:12) is easily identifiable in his phrase, "I have written to you…" With that, exhorting and testifying are perfect summations of Peter's objective in writing his letter. His exhortations/encouragements abound, spurring these Christians on through their hardships. And who better to testify to God's amazing grace than one of Jesus' closest friends and apostles? As you read and mark Peter's first letter, be mindful of the ways he encourages his readers and the information he provides regarding his firsthand knowledge of Jesus and the life He lived.

> "Through Silvanus, our faithful brother (for so I regard him), I have written to you briefly, exhorting and testifying that this is the true grace of God. Stand firm in it!" – 1 Peter 5:12

Suggestion: Underline this verse using a distinct color. (Orange?)

Marked: ☐   **My Mark:**

Notes:

PETITION VERBS

Peter's petition verb of choice is *parakaleō*. Most literal versions of the Bible translate this verb as *urge* in 1 Peter 2:11 and *exhort / exhorting* in 5:1 & 12. By using this verb, Peter is drawing special attention to his instructions in these passages. It is certainly fitting for *exhorting* to appear in the purpose statement, drawing our attention even closer to why he wrote this letter in the first place. If you'd like, list some of the things Peter is urging and exhorting his readers to do.

PETITION VERBS	REFERENCE	GREEK	TRANSLITERATION
URGE	2:11	παρακαλέω	*parakaleō*
EXHORT	5:1, 5:12	παρακαλέω	*parakaleō*

Suggestion: Mark these words with a distinct symbol. (?)
You may also choose to underline the entire verse.
Remember that 5:12 may already be underlined as Peter's purpose statement.

Marked: ☐   My Mark:

Notes:

THE WILL OF GOD

You've probably heard it shouted in some ridiculous movie: "It is the will of the gods!" or "It is God's will!" This is commonly followed by a person(s) doing something that would obviously not be "willed" to happen by the God we know and read about in Scripture. Peter, an inspired apostle of Jesus Christ, gives us a much clearer picture of what God's will actually is for His people with his recurring phrase, "the will of God."

"For such is the will of God"	2:15
"if God should will it so"	3:17
"but for the will of God"	4:2
"according to the will of God"	4:19

Suggestion: Underline these phrases with a distinct color. (Blue squiggly line?)

Marked: ☐   **My Mark:**

Study:

🔍 The New American Standard Bible includes other "will of God" phrases that other translations do not render as "the will of God." If you'd like, mark these phrases the same way as you did above.

"according to the will of God"	4:6
"according to the will of God"	5:2

Marked: ☐   **My Mark:**

Question:

📖 Consider the contexts of each of the phrases above regarding God's will. How does Peter develop the concept of God's will? Do these instances indicate that God is making bad things happen to His people? How do you know?

📖 What do you think Peter means when he discusses Christians suffering "according to the will of God"? (cf. 1 Peter 3:17; 4:19)

KEY WORDS

SUFFERING

It has been said that if you haven't suffered as a Christian, you haven't been one for long. Peter himself was no stranger to the intimidation and sufferings that came on behalf of his faith and proclamation of Jesus (e.g. Acts 4:21; 5:40-42; 12:1-3). Taught by his own experiences, Peter points his readers upward. He draws their attention to Christ and His sufferings at the hands of men throughout the letter (cf. 2:21-25; 3:17-18; 4:12-13). If He can do it – the just for the unjust – then we can do it too. As you mark *suffering*, pay very close attention to the details of these Christians' circumstances. To what degree do they seem to be *suffering*? Is it life or death? Insult for insult? Something else?

WORD	GREEK-R	TRANSLITERATION	OCCURRENCES	SUGGESTED SYMBOL
Suffering	πασχω	*paschō*	17	~~Suffering~~

Marked: ☐   **My Mark:**

1 Pet. 1:11	indicating as He predicted the	sufferings	of Christ and the glories to
1 Pet. 2:19	bears up under sorrows when	suffering	unjustly.
1 Pet. 2:20	when you do what is right and	suffer	*for it* you patiently endure it,
1 Pet. 2:21	this purpose, since Christ also	suffered	for you, leaving you an example
1 Pet. 2:23	did not revile in return; while	suffering	, He uttered no threats, but kept
1 Pet. 3:8	all of you be harmonious,	sympathetic	, brotherly, kindhearted, and
1 Pet. 3:14	But even if you should	suffer	for the sake of righteousness, *you*
1 Pet. 3:17	God should will it so, that you	suffer	for doing what is right rather
1 Pet. 3:18	For Christ also	died	for sins once for all, *the* just
1 Pet. 4:1	Therefore, since Christ has	suffered	in the flesh, arm yourselves also
1 Pet. 4:1	because he who has	suffered	in the flesh has ceased from sin,
1 Pet. 4:13	the degree that you share the	sufferings	of Christ, keep on rejoicing, so
1 Pet. 4:15	Make sure that none of you	suffers	as a murderer, or thief, or
1 Pet. 4:19	Therefore, those also who	suffer	according to the will of God shall
1 Pet. 5:1	and witness of the	sufferings	of Christ, and a partaker also of
1 Pet. 5:9	that the same experiences of	suffering	are being accomplished by your
1 Pet. 5:10	After you have	suffered	for a little while, the God of all

Study:

🔍 The word *suffering* is the most obvious thread through Peter's first letter that highlights the persecution of these Christians. However, there are many synonyms and descriptions of their *suffering* in the letter also. Make a list of all the words and phrases that describe the *suffering* of these saints [e.g. *slander* (2:12; 3:16) – *tested by fire* (1:7) – *intimidation* (3:14)]. After you've keyworded the rest of the book, you may want to mark these words to help them stand out as the modifiers of *suffering* (**Suggestion:** Gray squiggly line?).

Note: Be careful not to mark future key words like *evil/harm*, *unjustly*, etc. since they'll have their own symbols. Wait until you have keyworded the rest of the book before marking additional words.

Marked: ☐   **My Mark:**

Synonyms and descriptions of Christian *suffering*:

Question:

📖 Considering the list you compiled above and the overall theme of *suffering* in the letter, how would you describe the sufferings that these Christians are facing? Serious? Not serious? Somewhere in between?

📖 How would you describe the sufferings of Jesus that Peter recounted? In what ways do Jesus' sufferings set an "example" for Christians? (2:21)

📖 What might be an example of a Christian suffering for doing what is right? (cf. 2:19, 20; 3:14, 17)

📖 As you've already noticed, the root word for "sympathetic" in 1 Peter 3:8 is *paschō* (*suffering*). Given the context of the passage and the root meaning of the word, how would you describe what it means to be sympathetic? How might that look in these Christians' lives?

Notes:

DO

Christians have the divine endorsement to be the people who drive change on this planet. The world should follow God's people – not the other way around. To achieve this, Peter knows his readers must rise above their circumstances, not returning "evil for evil" (3:9). It will be difficult, but righteous conduct in every situation, especially sufferings, is what's going to turn a non-believer's head, while at the same time countering any assaults on their character. Christian behavior – "*doing* what is right" (4:19) – reflects God's nature and cause. Retaliation does not. If the world won't listen, then let it see. Before marking *do*, glance through the next two key words, *good* and *evil*, to get a feel for how you want to proceed. Notice that *do* and *evil* are both in the same word, *evildoer*. Consider the marking suggestions below.

WORD	GREEK-R	TRANSLITERATION	OCCURRENCES	SUGGESTED SYMBOL
Do	ποιεω	*poieō*	15	Do

evildoers   do evil   doing what is right

Marked: ☐   My Mark:

1 Pet. 2:9		A PEOPLE FOR God's	OWN	POSSESSION, so that you may
1 Pet. 2:12	in which they slander you as evil	doers	, they may because of your good
1 Pet. 2:14	for the punishment of evil	doers	and the praise of those who do
1 Pet. 2:14	and the praise of those who	do	right.
1 Pet. 2:15	such is the will of God that by	doing	right you may silence the
1 Pet. 2:20	it with patience? But if when you	do	what is right and suffer *for it*
1 Pet. 2:22	WHO	COMMITTED	NO SIN, nor was any deceit found
1 Pet. 3:6	have become her children if you	do	what is right without being
1 Pet. 3:11	TURN AWAY FROM EVIL AND	DO	GOOD; He must seek peace and
1 Pet. 3:12	OF THE LORD IS AGAINST THOSE WHO	DO	EVIL."
1 Pet. 3:17	will it so, that you suffer for	doing	what is right rather than for
1 Pet. 3:17	what is right rather than for	doing	what is wrong.
1 Pet. 3:18	put to death in the flesh, but	made	alive in the spirit;
1 Pet. 4:15	as a murderer, or thief, or evil	doer	, or a troublesome meddler;
1 Pet. 4:19	souls to a faithful Creator in	doing	what is right.

Study:

🔍 *Work* (*ergon*) is contextually related to *do* (*poieō*) in 1 Peter. If you'd like, mark this word (3x) with a similar symbol (see "Optional Words" for a symbol suggestion.) (*work* in 1:17 – *deeds* in 2:12 – *carried out* in 4:3.)

Marked: ☐ | **My Mark:**

🔍 Again, *do* is an important word to mark separately in Peter's first letter because it expresses the proactivity of faith. Specifics of Christian conduct – *doing* Christianity – will be discussed in the contexts of *good* and *evil* in the next few sections.

Notes:

GOOD

Everyday life makes it challenging enough to do *good*. Provocation from others makes it even harder. Just being human guarantees a certain amount of conflict with those around us, but what does God want us to do when people zero in on our lives and attempt to make us miserable for our faith in God? Do *right*. Do *Good*. And you will see good days (3:10). Peter urges his readers to keep their behavior *excellent*. The world is watching...today – tomorrow – until we pass from this life or the coming of Christ.

WORD	GREEK-R	TRANSLITERATION	OCCURRENCES	SUGGESTED SYMBOL
Good	αγαθος	*agathos*	13	Good

Marked: ☐   My Mark:

1 Pet. 2:14	the praise of those who do	right	.
1 Pet. 2:15	the will of God that by doing	right	you may silence the
1 Pet. 2:18	not only to those who are	good	and gentle, but also to those who
1 Pet. 2:20	But if when you do what is	right	and suffer *for it*
1 Pet. 3:6	her children if you do what is	right	without being
1 Pet. 3:10	DESIRES LIFE, TO LOVE AND SEE	GOOD	DAYS, MUST KEEP HIS TONGUE FROM
1 Pet. 3:11	TURN AWAY FROM EVIL AND DO	GOOD	; HE MUST SEEK PEACE AND PURSUE IT
1 Pet. 3:13	if you prove zealous for what is	good	?
1 Pet. 3:16	and keep a	good	conscience so that in the thing in
1 Pet. 3:16	those who revile your	good	behavior in Christ will be put to
1 Pet. 3:17	for doing what is	right	rather than for
1 Pet. 3:21	flesh, but an appeal to God for a	good	conscience—through the
1 Pet. 4:19	faithful Creator in doing what is	right	.

Study:

🔍 Although *agathos* is the primary word for *good/right* in his letter, Peter uses another word for *good* (*kalos*) that reveals another layer of thought regarding Christian conduct. Mark the references to *kalos* (3x) with a similar symbol as *agathos* (*excellent* in 2:12 – *good* in 2:12 & 4:10.)

Marked: ☐   My Mark:

🔍 Look up the definitions of *agathos* and *kalos* in your Bible dictionary. How do these words complement one another and aid your understanding of the theme of Christian conduct in Peter's first letter?

Definition of *agathos*:

Definition of *kalos*:

How *agathos* and *kalos* aid your understanding of the theme of Christian conduct:

🔍 Speaking of doing what is right, you may also want to mark the references to *righteousness* (*dikē*) in Peter's first letter (See "Optional Words" for a symbol suggestion.) Due to the large variety of lemma forms of the word (i.e. righteous, just, righteousness, righteously, unjustly, etc.) a root list will not be given here since it is optional. You can either use your Biblical concordance to locate all seven lemma forms of the word, *dikē*, or just mark *righteousness* / *just* as you find them in your translation.

Marked: ☐   My Mark:

Question:

📖 1 Peter 2:15 says, "For such is the will of God that by doing *right* you may silence the ignorance of foolish men." According to what you've studied so far in this letter, how do you suppose doing *right* will silence the ignorance of foolish men? (cf. 3:13, 16)

📖 What are some other benefits Peter gives that come with doing what is *right*?

📖 How do you discern what the *right* thing to do in troubling circumstances is?

📖 Would you say that you do what is *right* when you are mistreated? If yes, how? If not, what can you do to change that?

Notes:

EVIL

Exercising restraint after suffering an injustice is one of the most difficult and emotional undertakings for the Christian. After all, the world adamantly teaches that fair is fair – and a person is justified in taking swift revenge for any wrong. Passages like 1 Peter 2:1; 3:9-12; & 17 seem to indicate that these Christians are being tempted to fling evil right back in the faces of their antagonists. Peter likely had Jesus' words in Matthew 5:38-48 in mind as he discussed *evil* and its danger to Christian influence. If Christians respond the way the world responds to *evil*, what makes them different? The thought comes full circle in 5:8, when Peter reminds these Christians that the devil is trying to use their sufferings as an opportunity to lure them into *evil* and ultimately devour them. The remedy? Resist him! Run to God! He's the one who will "perfect, confirm, strengthen and establish you" (5:10).

WORD	GREEK-R	TRANSLITERATION	OCCURRENCES	SUGGESTED SYMBOL
Evil	κακος	*kakos*	12	Evil

Marked: ☐   **My Mark:**

1 Pet. 2:1	Therefore, putting aside all	malice	and all deceit and hypocrisy and
1 Pet. 2:12	in which they slander you as	evil	doers, they may because of your good
1 Pet. 2:14	the punishment of	evil	doers and the praise of those who do
1 Pet. 2:16	your freedom as a covering for	evil	, but *use it* as bondslaves of God.
1 Pet. 3:9	not returning	evil	for evil or insult for insult, but
1 Pet. 3:9	not returning evil for	evil	or insult for insult, but giving a
1 Pet. 3:10	MUST KEEP HIS TONGUE FROM	EVIL	AND HIS LIPS FROM SPEAKING DECEIT
1 Pet. 3:11	"HE MUST TURN AWAY FROM	EVIL	AND DO GOOD; HE MUST SEEK PEACE
1 Pet. 3:12	LORD IS AGAINST THOSE WHO DO	EVIL	."
1 Pet. 3:13	Who is there to	harm	you if you prove zealous for what
1 Pet. 3:17	rather than for doing what is	wrong	.
1 Pet. 4:15	as a murderer, or thief, or	evil	doer, or a troublesome meddler;

Study:

🔍 *Evil* is the most recurring word in 1 Peter that expresses wickedness. However, plenty of other words in his epistle bear the semblance of *evil* and wrongdoing. A few of them occur more than once or twice, such as: *sin* (8x) and *lust* (4x). If you'd like, mark the references to these words (See "Optional Words" for symbol suggestions.)

> *Sin* (*hamartanō*): 2:20, 22, 24 (2x); 3:18; 4:1, 8, & 18 (sinner)
>
> **Marked:** ☐ | **My Mark:**
>
> *Lust* (*epithymia*): 1:14; 2:11; 4:2, 3
>
> **Marked:** ☐ | **My Mark:**

🔍 If you'd like, make a list of words that appear in the same contexts as *evil*, *sin*, and *lust*. (e.g. *deceit*, etc. in 2:1, *sensuality*, etc. in 4:3, *murderer*, etc. in 4:15) After you've keyworded the rest of the book, you may want to mark these words to easily see the contrast between good and *evil* in the book (**Suggestion:** Red squiggly line?).

Marked: ☐ | **My Mark:**

Synonyms of evil, sin, and lust:

_____
_____
_____

Question:

📖 Consider your list of words above in light of the theme of *suffering*. What circumstances might be tempting these Christians to get involved with things like deceit, hypocrisy, envy, slander, thievery, etc.?

_____
_____
_____

📖 How would you summarize Peter's discussions concerning *evil*? What dynamics of *evil* seem to be heaviest on his mind?

_____
_____
_____

📖 What specific actions does Peter caution his readers to take regarding *evil*?

_____
_____
_____

GLORY

Peter's first letter is absolutely brimming with words of triumph. *Glory, honor, life, salvation, eternal, imperishable,* and so on. Don't miss the contrasts Peter makes between our life here and the glory awaiting us which is "reserved in heaven" (1:4). *Honor* is contextually related to *glory*, so it has been included in this section. 1 Peter 5:10 says, "After you have *suffered* for a little while, the God of all *grace*, who *called* you to His *eternal glory* in Christ, will Himself perfect, confirm, strengthen and establish you." If one remains totally committed and lives out his *faith* in Christ, come what may, he will receive the unfading crown of *glory* (5:4) (cf. James 1:12; 2 Tim. 4:6-8). What's Peter's point? Sufferings and trials of life are worth the *glory* to come! There's nothing the God of all creation wants more than to be with us forever!

WORD	GREEK-R	TRANSLITERATION	OCCURRENCES	SUGGESTED SYMBOL
Glory	δοκεω	*dokeō*	14	Glory

Marked: ☐   **My Mark:**

1 Pet. 1:7	be found to result in praise and	glory	and honor at the revelation of
1 Pet. 1:8	joy inexpressible and full of	glory	,
1 Pet. 1:11	the sufferings of Christ and the	glories	to follow.
1 Pet. 1:21	Him from the dead and gave Him	glory	, so that your faith and hope are
1 Pet. 1:24	FLESH IS LIKE GRASS, AND ALL ITS	GLORY	LIKE THE FLOWER OF GRASS. THE
1 Pet. 2:12	good deeds, as they observe *them*,	glorify	God in the day of visitation.
1 Pet. 4:11	so that in all things God may be	glorified	through Jesus Christ, to whom
1 Pet. 4:11	Jesus Christ, to whom belongs the	glory	and dominion forever and ever.
1 Pet. 4:13	also at the revelation of His	glory	you may rejoice with exultation.
1 Pet. 4:14	blessed, because the Spirit of	glory	and of God rests on you.
1 Pet. 4:16	is not to be ashamed, but is to	glorify	God in this name.
1 Pet. 5:1	and a partaker also of the	glory	that is to be revealed,
1 Pet. 5:4	receive the unfading crown of	glory	.
1 Pet. 5:10	who called you to His eternal	glory	in Christ, will Himself perfect,

WORD	GREEK-R	TRANSLITERATION	OCCURRENCES	SUGGESTED SYMBOL
Honor	τιμη	*timē*	9	Honor

Marked: ☐   **My Mark:**

1 Pet. 1:7	of your faith, *being*	more precious	than gold which is
1 Pet. 1:7	result in praise and glory and	honor	at the revelation of Jesus Christ;
1 Pet. 1:19	but with	precious	blood, as of a lamb unblemished
1 Pet. 2:4	by men, but is choice and	precious	in the sight of God,
1 Pet. 2:6	I LAY IN ZION A CHOICE STONE, A	PRECIOUS	CORNER *stone*,
1 Pet. 2:7	This	precious value	, then, is for you who believe;
1 Pet. 2:17		Honor	all people, love the brotherhood,
1 Pet. 2:17	love the brotherhood, fear God,	honor	the king.
1 Pet. 3:7	she is a woman; and show her	honor	as a fellow heir of the grace of

Study:

🔍 Definition of *glory* (*doxa*):

🔍 Definition of *honor* (*timē*):

🔍 Peter makes an interesting contrast between *glory* (*doxa*) and *shame* (*aischros*) in his first letter. He says in 4:16 that "if anyone suffers as a Christian, he is not to be *ashamed*, but is to *glorify* God in this name." If you'd like, mark the four references Peter makes to this word. (See "Optional Words" for a symbol suggestion.)

   Shame (*aischros*): 2:6 (*disappointed*); 3:16; 4:16; 5:2 (*sordid gain*)

Marked: ☐   **My Mark:**

🔍 Peter also discusses *glory* and *honor* in his second letter on a few occasions, but they are not key to that text. If you'd like, mark the references to those words as well.

Glory in 2 Peter (*doxa* & *prosdokaō*): 1:3, 17 (2x), 17 (*well-pleased*); 2:10 (*majesties*); 3:18

Marked: ☐ | My Mark:

Honor in 2 Peter (*timē*): 1:1 (*same kind*), 4 (*precious*), 17 (*honor*)

Marked: ☐ | My Mark:

Question:

📖 According to 1 Peter 2:12; 4:11, & 16, what are some ways in which Christians bring *glory* to God?

📖 Peter makes it clear that Christians have a heavenly *glory* awaiting them (e.g. 1:7; 5:1). Considering the definition of *glory* (*doxa*) above and the way Peter develops the concept, do you think there's a sense in which Christians experience a degree of God's *glory* in this life? (cf. 1:8) Why or why not?

📖 According to Peter, what things does God consider to be *precious* and worthy of *honor*?

📖 Which groups of people does Peter specifically designate to be honored? Why should Christians *honor* these people? (**Note:** Some instances of worthiness of *honor* may not actually use the word – e.g. *masters* in 2:18, *elders* in 5:5).

📖 Which people, if any, do you struggle to *honor* in your own life? Why?

Notes:

FAITH

A person can have a lot of things taken from them in this life. Jobs, comforts, relationships, etc. But spiritual elements like *faith* and *hope* can only be relinquished by an individual voluntarily – never forcibly taken. Peter's crowd is undoubtedly facing trying times and being forced to cope with loss and change as the societies surrounding them reject and ridicule them for their trust in God. It would give the adversary no greater joy than to use these circumstances to sap these Christians of any *faith* and *hope* they may be cherishing. The apostle reminds them that the "proof of their faith," although tested, is "more precious than gold" (1:7). And since Jesus has been raised from the dead, they too have a living *hope* to embrace amid such vexing trials (1:3).

WORD	GREEK-R	TRANSLITERATION	OCCURRENCES	SUGGESTED SYMBOL
Faith	πιστευω	*pisteuō*	12	Faith

Marked: ☐   **My Mark:**

1 Pet. 1:5	by the power of God through	faith	for a salvation ready to be
1 Pet. 1:7	so that the proof of your	faith	, *being* more precious than gold
1 Pet. 1:8	you do not see Him now, but	believe	in Him, you greatly rejoice with
1 Pet. 1:9	obtaining as the outcome of your	faith	the salvation of your souls.
1 Pet. 1:21	who through Him are	believers	in God, who raised Him from the
1 Pet. 1:21	and gave Him glory, so that your	faith	and hope are in God.
1 Pet. 2:6	AND HE WHO	BELIEVES	IN HIM WILL NOT BE DISAPPOINTED."
1 Pet. 2:7	value, then, is for you who	believe	; but for those who disbelieve,
1 Pet. 2:7	who believe; but for those who	disbelieve	, "THE STONE WHICH THE BUILDERS
1 Pet. 4:19	shall entrust their souls to a	faithful	Creator in doing what is right.
1 Pet. 5:9	But resist him, firm in *your*	faith	, knowing that the same
1 Pet. 5:12	Through Silvanus, our	faithful	brother (for so I regard *him*), I

WORD	GREEK-R	TRANSLITERATION	OCCURRENCES	SUGGESTED SYMBOL
Hope	ελπις	*elpis*	5	Hope

Marked: ☐   **My Mark:**

1 Pet. 1:3	us to be born again to a living	hope	through the resurrection of Jesus
1 Pet. 1:13	keep sober *in spirit*, fix your	hope	completely
1 Pet. 1:21	Him glory, so that your faith and	hope	are in God.
1 Pet. 3:5	times the holy women also, who	hoped	in God, used to adorn
1 Pet. 3:15	you to give an account for the	hope	that is in you, yet with

Study:

🔍 If you'd like, mark Peter's two references to *faith* in his second letter (2 Peter 1:1, 5).

Marked: ☐   **My Mark:**

🔍 Although *love* (*agapaō* – 9x / *philos* – 4x) is not included in this guide as a key word, you may want to mark references to it. (See "Optional Words" for symbol suggestions.) *Agapē* love is seen as an imperative on occasion (e.g. 1:22; 2:17; 4:8); suggesting that Peter also desires that his readers lean on one another in hard times.

> *Love* (*agapaō*): 1:8, 22 (*fervently love*); 2:11 (*Beloved*), 17; 3:10; 4:8 (2x), 4:12 (*Beloved*); 5:14

Marked: ☐   **My Mark:**

🔍 *Philos* love does not quite carry the weight of *agapē* love, but it is still a word of interest regarding the relationships between these Christians (and us by extension).

> *Love* (*philos*): 1:22 (*sincere love*); 3:8 (*brotherly*); 4:9 (*hospitable*); 5:14 (*kiss*)

Marked: ☐   **My Mark:**

Question:

📖 Based on what you've already studied in Peter's first letter, what do you think would be considered "proof" of a Christian's *faith*? (1 Peter 1:7)

📖 The concepts of *faith* and *hope* are undoubtedly related in Scripture. How would you explain the relationship between the two? (cf. 1 Peter 1:21)

📖 1 Peter 3:15 says, "but sanctify Christ as Lord in your hearts, always being ready to make a defense to everyone who asks you to give an account for the *hope* that is in you, yet with gentleness and reverence." How do you make your defense to people who ask you about the *hope* you have in Jesus?

Notes:

HOLY

Peter refers to his readers as aliens and strangers on this earth (1:1; 2:11). Christians know that this world is not their home – that maybe they're not supposed to get too cozy on this rock since they are only here temporarily. With that, their behavior is to be such that it turns the hearts of those who do not know God toward their creator. *Holiness*, being set apart as God's peculiar people, will do just that. "But like the *Holy* One who called you, be *holy* yourselves also in all *your* behavior" (1:15). As you mark this word, continue to watch how Peter crafts his theme of Christian conduct. *Holy* is only one of many words in this letter that describes a genuine Christian's way of life. *Called* and *chosen* are included in this section since they too reinforce the distinctiveness of God's wonderful people. If for no other reason, Christians shouldn't get cozy here because they have been *chosen* and *called* by God to their heavenly home.

WORD	GREEK-R	TRANSLITERATION	OCCURRENCES	SUGGESTED SYMBOL
Holy	αγιος	*hagios*	12	Holy

Marked: ☐   **My Mark:**

1 Pet. 1:2	of God the Father, by the	sanctifying	work of the Spirit, to obey Jesus
1 Pet. 1:12	preached the gospel to you by the	Holy	Spirit sent from heaven—things
1 Pet. 1:15	but like the	Holy	One who called you, be holy
1 Pet. 1:15	the Holy One who called you, be	holy	yourselves also in all *your*
1 Pet. 1:16	it is written, "YOU SHALL BE	HOLY	, FOR I AM HOLY."
1 Pet. 1:16	"YOU SHALL BE HOLY, FOR I AM	HOLY	."
1 Pet. 1:22	have in obedience to the truth	purified	your souls for a sincere love of
1 Pet. 2:5	up as a spiritual house for a	holy	priesthood, to offer up spiritual
1 Pet. 2:9	RACE, A royal PRIESTHOOD, A	HOLY	NATION, A PEOPLE FOR *God's* OWN
1 Pet. 3:2	as they observe your	chaste	and respectful behavior.
1 Pet. 3:5	in this way in former times the	holy	women also, who hoped in God
1 Pet. 3:15	but	sanctify	Christ as Lord in your hearts,

WORD	GREEK-L	TRANSLITERATION	OCCURRENCES	SUGGESTED SYMBOL
Called	καλέω	*kaleō*	6	Called

Marked: ☐   **My Mark:**

1 Pet. 1:15	but like the Holy One who	called	you, be holy yourselves also in
1 Pet. 2:9	the excellencies of Him who has	called	you out of darkness into His
1 Pet. 2:21	For you have been	called	for this purpose, since Christ
1 Pet. 3:6	just as Sarah obeyed Abraham,	calling	him lord, and you have become her
1 Pet. 3:9	a blessing instead; for you were	called	for the very purpose that you
1 Pet. 5:10	while, the God of all grace, who	called	you to His eternal glory in

WORD	GREEK-L	TRANSLITERATION	OCCURRENCES	SUGGESTED SYMBOL
Chosen	ἐκλεκτός	*eklektos*	4	Chosen

Marked: ☐   **My Mark:**

1 Pet. 1:1	Asia, and Bithynia, who are	chosen	
1 Pet. 2:4	has been rejected by men, but is	choice	and precious in the sight of God,
1 Pet. 2:6	"BEHOLD, I LAY IN ZION A	CHOICE	STONE, A PRECIOUS CORNER *stone*,
1 Pet. 2:9	But you are A	CHOSEN	RACE, A royal PRIESTHOOD, A HOLY

WORD	GREEK-L	TRANSLITERATION	OCC...	SUGGESTED SYMBOL
Chosen	συνεκλεκτός	*syneklektos*	1	Chosen

Marked: ☐   **My Mark:**

1 Pet. 5:13	She who is in Babylon,	chosen	together with you, sends you

Study:

- 🔍 The primary thrust of *holiness* (*hagios*) in Scripture has to do with being "set apart." Peter discusses *holiness* with his readers as if to say, "Be different! Be distinct so people know you belong to God!" And that makes sense given the rest of the themes he develops. In 1:15, Peter uses the word in the imperative sense – "be holy." In other words, it's not an option!

- 🔍 Look up the definitions of *called* (*kaleō*) and *chosen* (*eklektos*) in your Bible dictionary. How do these definitions complement the idea of *holiness* and enhance your understanding of God's desire for His people to be set apart to Him?

    Definition of *kaleō*:

    Definition of *eklektos*:

    How these concepts demonstrate God's desire for a "set-apart people":

Question:

- 📖 What other words and phrases in Peter's first letter signify the distinctiveness of God's people? (cf. 2:4-5, 9-11)

- 📖 Peter commands his readers to "be holy yourselves also in all *your* behavior" (1:15). Is your behavior characterized by *holiness*? How do you know?

Notes:

LIVE

If there's one thing Peter wants to make sure these Christians know, it's that they're going to make it! Tests of faith, suffering unjustly, slandered reputations - none of them matter! It's going to be worth it! The words below (*live, salvation, souls, forever,* and *imperishable*) reflect Peter's great theme of Christian assurance and life after death. Notice the contrasts Peter makes between these "forever words" and the things that will not last. As you mark these terms, look for their opposites. *Forever* vs. finite things – *Salvation* vs. unsaved – *Souls* vs. flesh – etc. See the study prompts below for more "Optional Words" that demonstrate Peter's development of this major theme and an important "marking announcement" before marking these words.

WORD	GREEK-R	TRANSLITERATION	OCCURRENCES	SUGGESTED SYMBOL
Live	ζαω	zaō	10	L̂ive

Marked: ☐   **My Mark:**

1 Pet. 1:3	caused us to be born again to a	living	hope through the resurrection of
1 Pet. 1:23	*that is*, through the	living	and enduring word of God.
1 Pet. 2:4	And coming to Him as to a	living	stone which has been rejected by
1 Pet. 2:5	you also, as	living	stones, are being built up as a
1 Pet. 2:24	so that we might die to sin and	live	to righteousness; for by His
1 Pet. 3:7	as a fellow heir of the grace of	life	, so that your prayers will not be
1 Pet. 3:10	For, "THE ONE WHO DESIRES	LIFE	, TO LOVE AND SEE GOOD DAYS, MUST
1 Pet. 3:18	put to death in the flesh, but made	alive	in the spirit;
1 Pet. 4:5	to Him who is ready to judge the	living	and the dead.
1 Pet. 4:6	in the flesh as men, they may	live	in the spirit according to *the*

WORD	GREEK-R	TRANSLITERATION	OCCURRENCES	SUGGESTED SYMBOL
Salvation	σωζω	*sōzō*	8	Salvation

Marked: ☐   **My Mark:**

1 Pet. 1:5	power of God through faith for a	salvation	ready to be revealed in the last
1 Pet. 1:9	as the outcome of your faith the	salvation	of your souls.
1 Pet. 1:10	As to this	salvation	, the prophets who prophesied
1 Pet. 2:2	by it you may grow in respect to	salvation	,
1 Pet. 3:20	few, that is, eight persons, were	brought safely	through *the* water.
1 Pet. 3:21	to that, baptism now	saves	you—not the removal of dirt
1 Pet. 4:4	*them* into the same excesses of	dissipation	, and they malign *you*;
1 Pet. 4:18	DIFFICULTY THAT THE RIGHTEOUS IS	SAVED	, WHAT WILL BECOME OF THE

WORD	GREEK-R	TRANSLITERATION	OCCURRENCES	SUGGESTED SYMBOL
Souls	ψυχω	*psychō*	6	Souls

Marked: ☐   **My Mark:**

1 Pet. 1:9	your faith the salvation of your	souls	.
1 Pet. 1:22	to the truth purified your	souls	for a sincere love of the
1 Pet. 2:11	lusts which wage war against the	soul	.
1 Pet. 2:25	the Shepherd and Guardian of your	souls	.
1 Pet. 3:20	in which a few, that is, eight	persons	, were brought safely through *the*
1 Pet. 4:19	will of God shall entrust their	souls	to a faithful Creator in doing

WORD	GREEK-R	TRANSLITERATION	OCCURRENCES	SUGGESTED SYMBOL
Forever	αιων	*aiōn*	6	<Forever>

Marked: ☐   **My Mark:**

1 Pet. 1:25	WORD OF THE LORD ENDURES	FOREVER	." And this is the word which was
1 Pet. 4:11	the glory and dominion	forever	and ever. Amen.
1 Pet. 4:11	dominion forever	and ever	. Amen.
1 Pet. 5:10	who called you to His	eternal	glory in Christ, will Himself
1 Pet. 5:11	To Him *be* dominion	forever	and ever. Amen.
1 Pet. 5:11	To Him *be* dominion forever	and ever	. Amen.

WORD	GREEK-L	TRANSLITERATION	OCC...	SUGGESTED SYMBOL
Imperishable	ἄφθαρτος	*aphthartos*	3	Imperishable

Marked: ☐   **My Mark:**

1 Pet. 1:4	an inheritance *which is*	imperishable	and undefiled and will not fade
1 Pet. 1:23	which is perishable but	imperishable	, *that is*, through the living and
1 Pet. 3:4	of the heart, with the	imperishable	quality of a gentle and quiet

Study:

🔍 You have probably already noticed that *dissipation* (4:4) is in the reference list for *salvation*. That's because it shares the same Greek root. However, it essentially means the exact opposite of *salvation* and is indicative of behavior that would cause one to lose their *salvation*. This is comparable to the fact that *disbelieve* is in the same root list as *believe/faith*. You can either mark this word the same as the rest of the words in the list, leave it unmarked, or develop a new symbol for it.

Marked: ☐   **My Mark:**

🔍 Make a list of other "forever words" in Peter's letter. Whether you mark them or not is up to you, but it will be handy to have this list to reference since this is such a major theme in the letter. (See "Optional Words" for a symbol suggestion for *enduring* should you choose to mark it.) Also, *reserved* (*tēreō*) has an assigned symbol in 2 Peter under *Judgment* should you decide to mark that reference as well.

Examples: *enduring* (*menō*) in 1:23, 25; 2:20 (2x) – *reserved* (*tēreō*) in 1:4 – *unfading* (*marainō*) in 1:4; 5:4

"Forever words" in 1 Peter:

Marked: ☐   My Mark:

🔍 With so many references to the *eternal*, it only makes sense that Peter also lists several temporary things in contrast. Among these terms are *flesh* (8x) and *perishable* (3x). Mark these words. (See "Optional Words" for symbol suggestions.)

Flesh (*sarx*): 1:24; 2:11; 3:18, 21; 4:1 (2x), 2, 6

Marked: ☐   My Mark:

Perishable (*phthartos*): 1:18, 23   (*apollymi*): 1:7

Marked: ☐   My Mark:

🔍 Make a list of other words in Peter's first letter that indicate a temporary nature.

Examples: *withers* (*xēros*) in 1:24 – *little while* (*oligos*) in 1:6; 5:10 – etc.

"Temporary terms" in 1 Peter:

Marked: ☐   My Mark:

Question:

📖 By now you've marked several words that have to do with both the *eternal* and the temporary. What seems to be the pattern with these terms? What things are *living* that will continue on? What things will come to an end and/or simply have much less value than that which is *living*?

📖 What concepts or verses in this section stood out to you the most? Why?

Notes:

GRACE

Peter discusses *grace* in a variety of ways, not the least of which is that of the gift of Heaven to those who remain steadfast. He does not discuss *grace* haphazardly, but carefully interweaves this promise of God throughout the letter so as to encourage these Christians even more. Consider how Peter uses the theology of God's *grace* to embolden his readers. This word could very well have fit under the "forever words" you marked in the last section, but the combination of its multiple occurrences and the richness of its theology warranted its own list. As you read Peter's first letter, consider how awesome God's *grace* is!

WORD	GREEK-L	TRANSLITERATION	OCCURRENCES	SUGGESTED SYMBOL
Grace	χάρις	*charis*	10	Grace

Marked: ☐   **My Mark:**

1 Pet. 1:2	be sprinkled with His blood: May	grace	and peace be yours in the fullest
1 Pet. 1:10	prophets who prophesied of the	grace	that *would come* to you made
1 Pet. 1:13	fix your hope completely on the	grace	to be brought to you at the
1 Pet. 2:19	For this *finds*	favor	, if for the sake of conscience
1 Pet. 2:20	patiently endure it, this *finds*	favor	with God.
1 Pet. 3:7	her honor as a fellow heir of the	grace	of life, so that your prayers will
1 Pet. 4:10	as good stewards of the manifold	grace	of God.
1 Pet. 5:5	OPPOSED TO THE PROUD, BUT GIVES	GRACE	TO THE HUMBLE.
1 Pet. 5:10	a little while, the God of all	grace	, who called you to His eternal
1 Pet. 5:12	testifying that this is the true	grace	of God. Stand firm in it!

Study:

🔍 Definition of *grace* (*charis*):

Question:

📖 What are some things Peter mentions that Christians can do (or how they can live) to find *favor* with God?

📖 Peter refers to the "true *grace* of God" in 1 Peter 5:12. Considering the themes you've already studied in this letter, what do you think the "true *grace* of God" is? (cf. 1 Peter 5:10-12)

📖 *Gift* (*charisma*) in 1 Peter 4:10 is in the same word family as *grace* (*charis*). Peter states that "As each one has received a special *gift*, employ it in serving one another as good stewards of the manifold *grace* of God." What gift(s) have you been given and how are you using it to serve others?

Notes:

BEHAVIOR

Remember that Peter's first letter is totally steeped in words pertaining to Christian conduct. *Behavior* is contextually related to a lot of words you've already marked, like: *do, work, good, evil, holy*, etc., not to mention *fear*, which is included in this section, and *submit*, which you'll mark later. Don't miss what Peter's point is in all of this. Christians are under the world's microscope. Nonbelievers are watching. If Christians constantly lash out and return evil for evil, then they are no different than anyone else. If Christians are seen doing wrong, why would anyone seek after their God? Witnessing to the lost aside, excellent *behavior* will simply keep one out of trouble. You may be accused of something, but if there is no truth to it, those who pointed the finger will stand in shame when the truth comes out (3:16). And it will come out, either before men in this life or God in the next.

WORD	GREEK-R	TRANSLITERATION	OCCURRENCES	SUGGESTED SYMBOL
Behavior	στρεφω	*strephō*	8	Behavior

Marked: ☐   **My Mark:**

1 Pet. 1:15	holy yourselves also in all *your*	behavior	;
1 Pet. 1:17	according to each one's work,	conduct	yourselves in fear during the time
1 Pet. 1:18	silver or gold from your futile	way of life	inherited from your
1 Pet. 2:12	Keep your	behavior	excellent among the Gentiles, so
1 Pet. 2:25	like sheep, but now you have	returned	to the Shepherd and Guardian of
1 Pet. 3:1	may be won without a word by the	behavior	of their wives,
1 Pet. 3:2	your chaste and respectful	behavior	.
1 Pet. 3:16	those who revile your good	behavior	in Christ will be put to shame.

WORD	GREEK-R	TRANSLITERATION	OCCURRENCES	SUGGESTED SYMBOL
Fear	φοβος	*phobos*	8	Fear

Marked: ☐   **My Mark:**

1 Pet. 1:17	one's work, conduct yourselves in	fear	during the time of your stay *on*
1 Pet. 2:17	all people, love the brotherhood,	fear	God, honor the king.
1 Pet. 2:18	to your masters with all	respect	, not only to those who are good
1 Pet. 3:2	as they observe your chaste and	respectful	behavior.
1 Pet. 3:6	do what is right without being	frightened	by any fear.
1 Pet. 3:14	*you are* blessed. AND DO NOT	FEAR	THEIR INTIMIDATION,
1 Pet. 3:14	blessed. AND DO NOT FEAR THEIR	INTIMIDATION	, AND DO NOT BE TROUBLED,
1 Pet. 3:15	in you, yet with gentleness and	reverence	;

Study:

🔍 It's no secret that Christians are under close inspection by the world, which isn't necessarily a bad thing. A Christian who lives a genuinely God-filled life will cause the onlookers to do a doubletake. Godly *behavior* can and will win people to the Lord in many cases. If you'd like, mark the word *observe* (*epopteuō*) in 2:12 and 3:2. (See "Optional Words" for a symbol suggestion.)

Marked: ☐   **My Mark:**

Question:

📖 In which circumstances does Peter specifically discuss non-believers *observing* the *behavior* of Christians? What results does he say Christians may bring about because of their *behavior* in these cases? Have you seen these results either in your own life or someone else's? When?

📖 What are some other positive results Peter says may come about because of how Christians *behave* and handle various situations? Do you actively try to live these principles out in your own life? If not, why?

📖 Read 1 Peter 2:21-24 again. What sort of *behavior* did Jesus model for all mankind while facing His crucifixion? What steps can you take to embody His example when experiencing your own suffering?

📖 How else is *fear* (*phobos*) translated in your Bible? How does this enhance your understanding of the Biblical concept of *fear*?

📖 In 1 Peter 1:17, the apostle says, "If you address as Father the One who impartially judges according to each one's work, conduct yourselves in *fear* during the time of your stay on *earth*." What do you suppose Peter means when he says, "conduct yourselves in fear"? Are we supposed to be afraid of God? Why or why not?

Notes:

SUBMIT

The world we live in commonly associates *submission* with weakness and defeat. Not so in Scripture. In fact, *submission* requires incredible spiritual strength and maturity. Since God has given us free will, we don't *have* to do anything. We don't *have* to *submit* to Him. We don't *have* to *obey* Jesus Christ. We don't *have* to follow His Word. But it's a good idea. Choices still have consequences. Peter presents scenario after scenario – instruction after instruction – that brings about positive results if we *submit* to what God would have us *submit* to. From personal life to family life to governmental authority, God desires that His people live out their *faith* in a way that honors Him and embodies His divine nature. One might even say that *submission* has a lot to do with Christian *behavior*!

WORD	GREEK-L	TRANSLITERATION	OCCURRENCES	SUGGESTED SYMBOL
Submit	ὑποτάσσω	*hypotassō*	6	Submit

Marked: ☐   **My Mark:**

1 Pet. 2:13			Submit	yourselves for the Lord's sake to
1 Pet. 2:18		Servants, be	submissive	to your masters with all respect,
1 Pet. 3:1		In the same way, you wives, be	submissive	to your own husbands so that even
1 Pet. 3:5		used to adorn themselves, being	submissive	to their own husbands;
1 Pet. 3:22		authorities and powers had been	subjected	to Him.
1 Pet. 5:5		You younger men, likewise, be	subject	to *your* elders; and all of you,

WORD	GREEK-R	TRANSLITERATION	OCCURRENCES	SUGGESTED SYMBOL
Obedient	ακουω	*akouō*	4	Obedient

Marked: ☐   **My Mark:**

1 Pet. 1:2	work of the Spirit, to	obey	Jesus Christ and be sprinkled with
1 Pet. 1:14	As	obedient	children, do not be conformed to
1 Pet. 1:22	Since you have in	obedience	to the truth purified your souls
1 Pet. 3:6	just as Sarah	obeyed	Abraham, calling him lord, and you

WORD	GREEK-R	TRANSLITERATION	OCCURRENCES	SUGGESTED SYMBOL
Disobedient	πειθω	*peithō*	4	~~Disobedient~~

Marked: ☐

My Mark:

1 Pet. 2:8	stumble because they are	disobedient	to the word, and to this *doom* they
1 Pet. 3:1	so that even if any *of them* are	disobedient	to the word, they may be won
1 Pet. 3:20	who once were	disobedient	, when the patience of God kept
1 Pet. 4:17	*be* the outcome for those who do	not obey	the gospel of God?

Question:

📖 Every time Peter uses the word, *submit*, he goes on to list the reasons and benefits of a Christian *submitting* to a source of authority. According to Peter, who are some people/entities that Christians should *submit* to? What are the benefits in those instances for a Christian to *submit* himself/herself?

📖 Is there ever a time when Christians should **not** *submit* to those things as presented by Peter? If yes, when? How do you decide? Is there anything else in God's Word that might support your decision? (cf. Acts 5:29)

📖 The Greek root word, *akouō* (seen as *obedience* in 1 Peter), is also the primary word for hearing/listening in the New Testament. How would you summarize the relationship between the Biblical principles of hearing God and obeying God?

📖 Since *submission/obedience* is such a major theme in Peter's first letter, it stands to reason that he would also discuss those who are *disobedient*. Look back at your markings of *disobedient*. Which groups does Peter list as being *disobedient*? What are some things these groups have in common?

📖 Peter discusses some very personal and difficult circumstances of *submission* that many Christians may find extremely challenging to deal with. Which circumstances of *submission* in 1 Peter stick out to you as particularly difficult? Are there cases in your own life when *submission* is particularly difficult? If yes, what steps can you take that might help you *submit* in these instances? What is Peter's advice about this?

Notes:

REVEALED

Peter was in the upper room with Jesus and heard the Lord say, "If I go and prepare a place for you, I will come again and receive you to Myself, that where I am, *there* you may be also." (John 14:3). Although this promise was made directly to the apostles, the rest of Scripture teaches us that Jesus is coming again for all His faithful. The Lord will *reveal* Himself on that great day. If nothing else Peter says encourages these Christians, this should do it. Jesus has not abandoned His people. He's coming. And it will be known by the whole world that He is Lord of all (cf. 2 Thess. 1:7). The wrongs of the world will be made right. The unfading crown of glory will rest on the heads of the faithful. "And though you have not seen Him, you love Him, and though you do not see Him now, but believe in Him, you greatly rejoice with joy inexpressible and full of glory" (1 Peter 1:8).

WORD	GREEK-L	TRANSLITERATION	OCC...	SUGGESTED SYMBOL
Revealed	ἀποκαλύπτω	*apokaluptō*	3	Revealed

Marked: ☐   My Mark:

1 Pet. 1:5	faith for a salvation ready to be	revealed	in the last time.
1 Pet. 1:12	It was	revealed	to them that they were not serving
1 Pet. 5:1	also of the glory that is to be	revealed	,

WORD	GREEK-L	TRANSLITERATION	OCC...	SUGGESTED SYMBOL
Revelation	ἀποκάλυψις	*apokalypsis*	3	Revelation

Marked: ☐   My Mark:

1 Pet. 1:7	praise and glory and honor at the	revelation	of Jesus Christ;
1 Pet. 1:13	grace to be brought to you at the	revelation	of Jesus Christ.
1 Pet. 4:13	on rejoicing, so that also at the	revelation	of His glory you may rejoice with

WORD	GREEK-L	TRANSLITERATION	OCCURRENCES	SUGGESTED SYMBOL
Appeared	φανερόω	*phaneroō*	2	Appeared

Marked: ☐   **My Mark:**

1 Pet. 1:20	foundation of the world, but has	appeared	in these last times for the sake
1 Pet. 5:4	And when the Chief Shepherd	appears	, you will receive the unfading

Study:

🔍 Definition of *apokalyptō*:

Definition of *phaneroō*:

Question:

📖 What good things does Peter say will accompany the *revelation* of Christ? What will be the response of those who are ready for this day?

📖 Is Christ's return a comforting prospect for you? Why or why not?

Notes:

OPTIONAL WORDS

Remember that Optional Words are those words that are of some interest but may not be marked for a few different reasons: (1) they may not be exceedingly theologically significant, (2) they may be used so frequently that to mark them would mean making your Bible pages extremely crowded or too busy to focus on the other words marked, or (3) they may just be synonyms to the key words. It is up to your discretion whether or not to mark these words. Should you choose to mark any or all of these words, a Biblical concordance can help you find their occurrences in the original language.

WORD	TRANSLITERATION	OCC...	SUGGESTED SYMBOL	MARKED
God	*theos*	39	God	☐
Christ	*Christos*	23	Christ	☐
Righteousness	*dikē*	10	Righteousness	☐
Jesus	*Iēsous*	9	Jesus	☐
Lord	*kyrios*	9	Lord	☐
Love	*agapaō*	9	Love	☐
Sin	*hamartanō*	8	Sin	☐
Flesh	*sarx*	8	Flesh	☐
Shame	*aischros*	4	Shame	☐
Love	*philos*	4	Love	☐
Lust	*epithymia*	4	Lust	☐
Enduring	*menō*	4	Enduring	☐
Work	*ergon*	3	Work	☐
Perishable	*phthartos/apollymi*	3	Perishable	☐
Observe	*epopteuō*	2	Observe	☐

My Mark:	My Mark:
My Mark:	My Mark:
My Mark:	My Mark:
My Mark:	My Mark:
My Mark:	My Mark:
My Mark:	My Mark:
My Mark:	My Mark:
My Mark:	My Mark:

Notes:

KEY CONCLUSIONS

THEME OF 1 PETER:

MAJOR TOPICS IN 1 PETER:

APPLICATIONS FROM 1 PETER:

MY KEY WORDS

If you found some words that you think are key to the text but are not listed, list them below and assign them a symbol if you wish!

WORD	CHAPTER(S)	OCCURRENCES	SYMBOL	MARKED
				☐
				☐
				☐
				☐
				☐
				☐
				☐
				☐
				☐
				☐
				☐
				☐
				☐
				☐

"For no prophecy was ever made by an act of human will, but men moved by the Holy Spirit spoke from God."

2 Peter 1:21

2 PETER

STUDYING 2 PETER

1. Read the introduction to one of these guides at least once.
2. Read the "General Information" page to orient yourself to Peter's second epistle.
3. Read 2 Peter all the way through several times to familiarize yourself with the text.
4. Follow the directions found under "Key Concepts." This section will have you mark other important things prior to keywording the book.
5. Keyword the book:
    a. Turn to the first keywording page (e.g. *Knowledge*) and locate the suggested symbol for that particular word.
    b. Use the reference list provided in order to locate the English words in your Bible that correspond to their respective Greek word.
    c. Mark the located word with the suggested symbol. Do this for all the key words provided in each guide.
    d. When applicable, answer the questions and/or follow the study prompts included for the words.
    e. For an even deeper study of the word, define it using a reputable Bible dictionary.
6. Mark the Optional Words at your own discretion using the suggested symbols or by creating your own.
7. Complete the "Key Conclusions" section.
8. Utilize the "My Key Words" section when applicable.

GENERAL INFORMATION

AUTOR PETER THE APOSTLE
"Simon Peter, a bond-servant and apostle of Jesus Christ," (1:1)

GENRE GENERAL EPISTLE

DATE c. 67 A.D.

WRITTEN FR. ROME

RECIPIENTS TO THOSE WHO HAVE RECEIVED A FAITH OF THE SAME KIND AS OURS (1:1)
According to 2 Peter 3:1-2, Peter writes to the same group of Christians he addressed in his first letter – "the second letter I am writing to you…"

OCCASION Based on his own language and Jesus' indication decades earlier, it's a fair conclusion that Peter spent his final days in Roman custody (2 Peter 1:14-15; John 21:18-19). His parting words to the churches he had become so endeared to are not filled with sorrow and mourning over his impending death, but confidence that these Christians will be ready for any spiritual challenges they are faced with. False teachers with alluring promises and dangerous rhetoric will seek an audience with them, but Peter assures these Christians that they already possess the true knowledge of God. Nothing else is needed but to cling to the simplicity of Christ.

KEY CONCEPTS

PURPOSE STATEMENT

There are two passages in Peter's second letter that confirm his purpose for writing to these Christians a second time (1:12-15 and 3:1-2). And the purpose is simple: remember. Remember what you were taught. Remember the words of Jesus, His apostles, and the prophets. If you're beginning to forget, here's another reminder. Every reference to the word *remember/remind* (*mimnēskomai* – 5x) in 2 Peter occurs in these two passages. As you read and mark 2 Peter, look for the many reasons why he so strongly desires for his readers to *remember* the things they learned and knew to be true when they first came to believe in Christ.

> "Therefore, I will always be ready to remind you of these things, even though you *already* know *them*, and have been established in the truth which is present with *you*. I consider it right, as long as I am in this *earthly* dwelling, to stir you up by way of reminder, knowing that the laying aside of my *earthly* dwelling is imminent, as also our Lord Jesus Christ has made clear to me. And I will also be diligent that at any time after my departure you will be able to call these things to mind." – 2 Peter 1:12-15

> "This is now, beloved, the second letter I am writing to you in which I am stirring up your sincere mind by way of reminder, that you should remember the words spoken beforehand by the holy prophets and the commandment of the Lord and Savior *spoken* by your apostles." – 2 Peter 3:1-2

Suggestion: Underline these verses using a distinct color. (Orange?)

Marked: ☐   My Mark:

WORD	GREEK-R	TRANSLITERATION	OCC...	SUGGESTED SYMBOL
Remind	μιμνησκομαι	*mimnēskomai*	5	Remind

Marked: ☐ **My Mark:**

2 Pet. 1:12	I will always be ready to	remind	you of these things, even
2 Pet. 1:13	to stir you up by way of	reminder	,
2 Pet. 1:15	will be able to call these things	to mind	.
2 Pet. 3:1	up your sincere mind by way of	reminder	,
2 Pet. 3:2	that you should	remember	the words spoken

Study:

🔍 Even though you have not yet keyworded 2 Peter, list some things that you already see in the purpose statements that Peter is trying to *remind* his readers of. What are "these things" in 1:12, 15? (cf. 2 Peter 1:5-11)

Notes:

II PETER & JUDE

Given the obvious similarities in wording and subject matter, it is certain that both Peter and the Lord's brother, Jude, wrote to the same groups of believers at about the same time – Peter writing his second letter in approximately A.D. 67 and Jude his about two years later in A.D. 69. This sequence of events is in total harmony with what the textual evidence suggests. For his part, Peter writes almost entirely in the future tense concerning the arrival of the false teachers (e.g. "there **will also be** false teachers among you" (2:1) – "they **will exploit** you" (2:3) – "mockers **will come**" (3:3) – etc.). Conversely, Jude writes of these men in the present and past tense, indicating that they have already arrived (e.g. "certain persons **have crept** in" (4) – "these men **revile**" (10) – etc.). This same point has already been discussed in the *James & Jude Bible Keywording Guide*, but it is worth mentioning here again because of the close textual relationship between 2 Peter and Jude. If you'd like, compare the verses below and note some of their similarities. **NOTE:** This same chart is given in the *James & Jude Bible Keywording Guide* (p. 87).

JUDE	2 PETER	SIMILARITIES
4	2:1	
4	2:3	
6	2:4	
7	2:6	
8	2:10	
9	2:11	
10	2:12	
11	2:15	
12	2:13	
12	2:17	
13	2:17	
16	2:18	
17	3:2	
18	3:3	

Notes:

APPLYING ALL DILIGENCE

Peter's key words certainly develop the thought and flow of his second letter, but one of the concepts that is not knit together through common Greek root words is that of Christian diligence. Although *diligence* (*speudō*) does occur five times in this short letter, the concept is broader than five verses. The list below contains many of the phrases Peter uses to ensure that his readers are alert and ready for the inevitable attacks Satan will launch against their faith. The apostle has already used this "diligence terminology" in his first letter (e.g. "prepare your minds for action" (1 Peter 1:13) – "ready to make a defense" (3:15) – "Be of sober *spirit*, be on the alert" (5:8) – etc.). If you find more phrases that you believe should be included but are not in this list, use the blank spaces at the end to add them. Mark these phrases with a distinctive strikethrough or other symbol if you wish (**remember** to always be careful about symbol overlap with the key words of the book – In this case, be mindful of the already underlined purpose statements and the words: *remind/mind* (1:13, 15; 3:1, 2) – *sincere* (3:1) – *words/spoken* (3:2) – & *knowledge* (3:18).

NOTE: Peter only uses seven imperatives in this letter, and all seven of them have to do with Christian diligence. The imperatives are noted next to their respective references in the chart below. If you have a specific marking for imperatives, use it here in conjunction with your mark of choice for the rest of the references below.

My Mark - IMPERATIVES: ☐

PHRASE	REFERENCE	MARKED
"applying all diligence"	1:5	☐
"supply moral excellence" [IMPERATIVE]	1:5	☐
"and are increasing"	1:8	☐
"be all the more diligent to make certain" [IMPERATIVE]	1:10	☐
"practice these things"	1:10	☐
"I will always be ready"	1:12	☐
"to stir you up by way of reminder"	1:13	☐
"I will also be diligent"	1:15	☐
"able to call these things to mind"	1:15	☐
"pay attention"	1:19	☐

"I am stirring up your sincere mind by way of reminder"	3:1	☐
"you should remember the words"	3:2	☐
"<u>do not let</u> this one *fact* escape your notice" [IMPERATIVE]	3:8 cf. 3:5	☐
"looking for and hastening"	3:12	☐
"we are looking for"	3:13	☐
"look for these things"	3:14	☐
"<u>be diligent</u>" [IMPERATIVE]	3:14	☐
"<u>regard</u> the patience of our Lord" [IMPERATIVE]	3:15	☐
"<u>be on your guard</u>" [IMPERATIVE]	3:17	☐
"your own steadfastness"	3:17	☐
"<u>grow</u> in the grace and knowledge" [IMPERATIVE]	3:18	☐
		☐
		☐
		☐
		☐
		☐

Suggestion: Strikethrough these verses using a distinct color. (Green?)

My Mark:

Notes:

KEY WORDS

KNOWLEDGE

Knowledge is the undisputed front-running key word in Peter's second letter. Given that Peter devotes much of this letter to warnings regarding false prophets and teachers, it is no wonder that he emphasizes the *true knowledge* of God. If these Christians *know* and call to memory the things spoken by the Lord, His true apostles, and the genuine prophets of antiquity, then they will easily ascertain God's truth amid the erroneous words spoken by deceitful men. Don't miss Peter's lesson about the benefits of reminders and listening to the truth over and over again even though you've already heard it once. "Therefore, I will always be ready to remind you of these things, even though you *already* **know** them, and have been established in the truth which is present with *you*." (2 Peter 1:12; cf. 1:13-15)

WORD	GREEK-R	TRANSLITERATION	OCCURRENCES	SUGGESTED SYMBOL
Knowledge	γινωσκω	*ginōskō*	14	Knowledge

Marked: ☐   **My Mark:**

2 Pet. 1:2	peace be multiplied to you in the	knowledge	of God and of Jesus our Lord;
2 Pet. 1:3	and godliness, through the true	knowledge	of Him who called us by His own
2 Pet. 1:5	and in *your* moral excellence,	knowledge	,
2 Pet. 1:6	and in *your*	knowledge	, self-control, and in *your*
2 Pet. 1:8	nor unfruitful in the true	knowledge	of our Lord Jesus Christ.
2 Pet. 1:16	cleverly devised tales when we	made known	to you the power and coming
2 Pet. 1:20	But	know	this first of all, that no
2 Pet. 2:12	reviling where they have no	knowledge	, will in the destruction
2 Pet. 2:20	defilements of the world by the	knowledge	of the Lord and Savior Jesus
2 Pet. 2:21	be better for them not to have	known	the way of righteousness, than
2 Pet. 2:21	way of righteousness, than having	known	it, to turn away from the holy
2 Pet. 3:3		Know	this first of all, that in the
2 Pet. 3:17	You therefore, beloved,	knowing	this beforehand, be on your guard
2 Pet. 3:18	but grow in the grace and	knowledge	of our Lord and Savior Jesus

WORD	GREEK-R	TRANSLITERATION	OCCURRENCES	SUGGESTED SYMBOL
Know	οιδα	*oida*	3	Know

Marked: ☐   **My Mark:**

2 Pet. 1:12	things, even though you *already*	know	*them*, and have been established
2 Pet. 1:14		knowing	that the laying aside of my
2 Pet. 2:9	*then* the Lord	knows	how to rescue the godly from

Study:

🔍 It seems that the false teachers Peter warns his readers about are touting a special *knowledge* that only they have been enlightened with. Peter cautions these Christians that "no prophecy of Scripture is a *matter* of one's own interpretation, for no prophecy was ever made by an act of human will, but men moved by the Holy Spirit spoke from God" (2 Peter 1:20-21) (cf. 2:1; 3:16). God's truth is revealed through inspired individuals and not through people who offer their own take on things. Additional prophecies and secret teachings are not only unwarranted, but are actually "destructive" according to Peter. If you'd like, mark Peter's references to *truth* (*alētheia*) and *right* (*euthus*). (See "Optional Words" for symbol suggestions.)

Truth (*alētheia*): 1:12; 2:2, 22

Marked: ☐   **My Mark:**

Right (*euthus*): 2:15

Marked: ☐   **My Mark:**

🔍 If you'd like, make a list of all the things Peter says that these Christians have a *knowledge* of for your future reference.

These Christians have a knowledge of:

🔍 Peter uses the word *know* (*oida*) twice in his first letter (1 Peter 1:18; 5:9). If you'd like, mark these references with the same symbol.

Marked: ☐   **My Mark:**

Question:

📖 Amid Peter's discussions of the importance of the *knowledge* of Christ, he makes reference to those who are *untaught* and *unstable* (2:14; 3:16) who "live in error" (2:18; 3:17). According to Peter, what are some of the dangers of both being these things and listening to those who do not have the true *knowledge* of God?

📖 How does Peter's reference to being with Jesus "on the holy mountain" reinforce his credibility and reveal his *knowledge* of Christ? (2 Peter 1:16-18). Why would this be an important event to recount when refuting false teachers?

📖 Speaking of the false teachers in 2:21, Peter says, "For it would be better for them not to have *known* the way of righteousness, than having *known* it, to turn away from the holy commandment handed on to them." How would having the knowledge of Jesus and then turning away from it be worse for them than the first? (cf. Luke 12:47-48).

📖 Do you know anyone who has had the *knowledge* of Christ and *known* the way of righteousness who has turned away from the faith? What seemed to have led them astray?

📖 Peter mentions in 3:15-16 that the Apostle Paul had also written at least one letter to these Christians (probably more) and says that some things he discusses are "hard to understand." How do you handle difficult passages you read in God's Word?

Notes:

DESTRUCTION

The ancient Greeks had many words for *destruction*, and Peter used no fewer than four of them in this letter, all with a slight nuance. Peter pulls no punches in using these words to paint a vivid picture of what awaits those who devote their lives to luring God's people from His fold. *Destruction* is no respecter of persons. Peter issues examples of past *destruction* (rebellious angels, Noah's contemporaries, Sodom and Gomorrah, etc.) and future *destruction* for those who continue in *ungodliness* (e.g. 3:7). He even speaks of it in the present tense – meaning while the person is still living (e.g. 2:1 – "bringing swift destruction upon themselves"). This is reminiscent of Paul's words in 1 Timothy 1:19 when he describes certain blasphemers as having "suffered shipwreck in regard to their faith." Don't miss God's steadfast love in the midst of such a negative concept. "The Lord is not slow about His promise, as some count slowness, but is patient toward you, not wishing for any to *perish* but for all to come to repentance" (2 Peter 3:9).

WORD	GREEK-R	TRANSLITERATION	OCC...	SUGGESTED SYMBOL
Destruction	ολεθρος	olethros	7	Destruction

Marked: ☐   **My Mark:**

2 Pet. 2:1	you, who will secretly introduce	destructive	heresies, even denying the Master
2 Pet. 2:1	who bought them, bringing swift	destruction	upon themselves.
2 Pet. 2:3	long ago is not idle, and their	destruction	is not asleep.
2 Pet. 3:6	which the world at that time was	destroyed	, being flooded with water.
2 Pet. 3:7	kept for the day of judgment and	destruction	of ungodly men.
2 Pet. 3:9	you, not wishing for any to	perish	but for all to come to repentance.
2 Pet. 3:16	of the Scriptures, to their own	destruction	.

WORD	GREEK-R	TRANSLITERATION	OCC…	SUGGESTED SYMBOL
Destruction	φθειρω	*phtheirō*	5	Destruction

Marked: ☐   **My Mark:**

2 Pet. 1:4	divine nature, having escaped the	corruption	that is in the world by lust.
2 Pet. 2:12	of instinct to be captured and	killed	, reviling where they have no
2 Pet. 2:12	have no knowledge, will in the	destruction	of those creatures also be
2 Pet. 2:12	of those creatures also be	destroyed	,
2 Pet. 2:19	they themselves are slaves of	corruption	; for by what a man is overcome,

WORD	GREEK-L	TRANSLITERATION	OCC…	SUGGESTED SYMBOL
Destroyed	λύω	*luō*	3	Destroyed

Marked: ☐   **My Mark:**

2 Pet. 3:10	a roar and the elements will be	destroyed	with intense heat, and the earth
2 Pet. 3:11	Since all these things are to be	destroyed	in this way, what sort of people
2 Pet. 3:12	of which the heavens will be	destroyed	by burning, and the elements will

WORD	GREEK-L	TRANSLITERATION	OCC…	SUGGESTED SYMBOL
Destruction	καταστροφή	*katastrophē*	1	Destruction

Marked: ☐   **My Mark:**

2 Pet. 2:6	cities of Sodom and Gomorrah to	destruction	by reducing *them* to ashes, having

Question:

📖 Peter discusses *destruction* in a variety of contexts and ultimately shows the concept to be multi-dimensional (i.e. it's not just physical, something that only happened in the past, etc.). What are some key descriptions Peter gives of *destruction* that make it such a terrifying thing?

📖 According to Peter, the false teachers are known for distorting the Scriptures to "their own destruction" (3:16) and will attempt to "secretly introduce destructive heresies" (2:1). Having read the letter through and marked the references to *destruction*, what do you think is the nature of the *destructive* heresies that they are trying to introduce to these Christians? (cf. 2:18-19 esp.)

📖 What do you suppose Peter means when he says that "their judgment from long ago is not idle, and their *destruction* is not asleep" in 2:3?

Notes:

DAY

We don't know every detail about the heresies that the false teachers were going to attempt to introduce to God's people in Peter's day, but it is clear that a denial of the Lord's return was a cornerstone of their falsity (2 Peter 3:4). If you can convince someone that God will not hold them accountable for their actions, then there's no limit to the immorality and lawlessness they may engage in. But Peter sees this coming. He reminds these Christians that there is a day and the Lord is not slow about keeping His appointment. "But the day of the Lord will come like a thief, in which the heavens will pass away with a roar and the elements will be destroyed with intense heat, and the earth and its works will be burned up" (2 Peter 3:10)

WORD	GREEK-R	TRANSLITERATION	OCCURRENCES	SUGGESTED SYMBOL
Day	ημερα	hēmera	12	Day

Marked: ☐   **My Mark:**

2 Pet. 1:19	in a dark place, until the	day	dawns and the morning star arises
2 Pet. 2:8	felt *his* righteous soul tormented	day	after day by *their* lawless deeds),
2 Pet. 2:8	righteous soul tormented day after	day	by *their* lawless deeds),
2 Pet. 2:9	under punishment for the	day	of judgment,
2 Pet. 2:13	it a pleasure to revel in the	daytime	. They are stains and blemishes,
2 Pet. 3:3	first of all, that in the last	days	mockers will come with *their*
2 Pet. 3:7	reserved for fire, kept for the	day	of judgment and destruction of
2 Pet. 3:8	beloved, that with the Lord one	day	is like a thousand years, and a
2 Pet. 3:8	and a thousand years like one	day	.
2 Pet. 3:10	But the	day	of the Lord will come like a
2 Pet. 3:12	and hastening the coming of the	day	of God, because of which the
2 Pet. 3:18	*be* the glory, both now and to the	day	of eternity. Amen.

WORD	GREEK-L	TRANSLITERATION	OCCURRENCES	SUGGESTED SYMBOL
Coming	παρουσία	*parousia*	3	Coming ⬇

Marked: ☐   **My Mark:**

2 Pet. 1:16	known to you the power and	coming	of our Lord Jesus Christ, but we
2 Pet. 3:4	"Where is the promise of His	coming	? For *ever* since the fathers fell
2 Pet. 3:12	looking for and hastening the	coming	of the day of God, because of

Study:

🔍 Remember that Peter also devotes a lot of ink in his first letter demonstrating that Jesus is coming back for His faithful ones. His repeated references to that which will be *revealed* and to the *appearing* and *revelation* of Jesus Christ totally undermines the premise of the false teachers that there is no *Day of the Lord*. Revisit the key word *Revealed* in 1 Peter for a refresher and mark the phrase "day of visitation" in 1 Peter 2:12 with your symbol for *Day* if you wish.

Marked: ☐   **My Mark:**

Question:

📖 Peter speaks at length about Christ's return in both of his letters. What do you think are some of the major differences between his reasons for writing about that *Day* in his first letter compared to that of his second?

📖 Why do you think that mocking and disparaging the *coming* of the *Day* of Judgment was a major platform for the false teachers? (cf. 3:3-4).

📖 What was the main argument the false teachers used to "prove" that Jesus isn't coming? (cf. 3:4)

📖 What facts does Peter remind these Christians of that actually prove Jesus is *coming* and that the *Day* of the Lord is a reality to be faced? (cf. 3:5-10)

Notes:

RIGHTEOUS

One of the most obvious contrasts in 2 Peter is that between *righteousness* and *unrighteousness*. This contrast is also seen throughout the letter in *godliness* versus *ungodliness* (to be marked a few sections later). Perhaps the most comforting lesson Peter teaches us with this word is that God knows those who are His and won't abandon them. In the jumble of global wickedness, God zooms in and finds the one *righteous* man left on earth – "Noah, a preacher of *righteousness*" (2:5). Years later, God rescues Lot, the last *righteous* man in the bustling cities of Sodom and Gomorrah (2:6-8). "*Then* the Lord knows how to rescue the *godly* from temptation, and to keep the *unrighteous* under punishment for the day of judgment" (2:9).

WORD	GREEK-L	TRANSLITERATION	OCCURRENCES	SUGGESTED SYMBOL
Righteous	δίκαιος	*dikaios*	4	Righteous

Marked: ☐   **My Mark:**

2 Pet. 1:13	I consider it	right	, as long as I am in this *earthly*
2 Pet. 2:7	and *if* He rescued	righteous	Lot, oppressed by the sensual
2 Pet. 2:8	by what he saw and heard *that*	righteous	man, while living among them, felt
2 Pet. 2:8	while living among them, felt *his*	righteous	soul tormented day after day by

WORD	GREEK-L	TRANSLITERATION	OCC...	SUGGESTED SYMBOL
Righteousness	δικαιοσύνη	*dikaiosynē*	4	Righteousness

Marked: ☐   **My Mark:**

2 Pet. 1:1	of the same kind as ours, by the	righteousness	of our God and Savior, Jesus
2 Pet. 2:5	but preserved Noah, a preacher of	righteousness	, with seven others, when He
2 Pet. 2:21	not to have known the way of	righteousness	, than having known it, to turn
2 Pet. 3:13	heavens and a new earth, in which	righteousness	dwells.

WORD	GREEK-L	TRANSLITERATION	OCC...	SUGGESTED SYMBOL
Unrighteousness	ἀδικία	*adikia*	2	Unrighteousness

Marked: ☐   **My Mark:**

2 Pet. 2:13	wrong as the wages of	doing wrong	. They count it a pleasure to
2 Pet. 2:15	of Beor, who loved the wages of	unrighteousness	;

WORD	GREEK-L	TRANSLITERATION	OCC...	SUGGESTED SYMBOL
Unrighteous	ἄδικος	*adikos*	1	Unrighteous

Marked: ☐   **My Mark:**

2 Pet. 2:9	temptation, and to keep the	unrighteous	under punishment for the day

WORD	GREEK-L	TRANSLITERATION	OCC...	SUGGESTED SYMBOL
Suffering wrong	ἀδικέω	*adikeō*	1	Suffering wrong

Marked: ☐   **My Mark:**

2 Pet. 2:13		suffering wrong	as the wages of doing wrong.

Study:

- 🔍 Since there is such an obvious contrast between *righteousness/godliness* and *unrighteousness/ungodliness* in this letter, lists of synonyms to these words should be made. Space for the list of *unrighteous/ungodly* terms will be included under this section, and space for the list of *righteous/godly* terms will be included under the key word *Godliness* a few sections later.

- 🔍 Like Jude, Peter uses many terms to describe the false teachers. After you mark his uses of *unrighteous* and *ungodly* (to be marked a few sections later), you may want to go back through this letter and begin making a list of other synonyms that reveal the depravity of these individuals. Once you have keyworded the rest of the book, you may want to refer back to this list of descriptions and shade them with the color of your choice. (**Note:** There are **several** of these terms in chapter two. If you choose to shade them, realize that it will be the dominant color on the page).

Examples: *sensuality (2:2) – greed (2:3) – indulge the flesh, corrupt desires, despise authority, daring, self-willed, do not tremble, revile angelic majesties (2:10) – unprincipled men (2:7; 3:17) – etc.*

Marked: ☐   My Mark:

Actions and Descriptions of the false teachers:

Question:

- We're told in Genesis 13:8-13 that Lot voluntarily chose to move he and his family to Sodom. Peter describes Lot's experience as a *righteous* man in Sodom to be that of oppression and torment because of "what he saw and heard" (2:7-8). What lessons are there in this account for us as God's people today?

- Peter describes Balaam as one who "loved the wages of *unrighteousness*" in 2:15. Refer back to the account of Balaam in Numbers 22-24; 31:8, 16. What did Balaam stand to gain through his unrighteousness? How does this compare to the false teachers of Peter's time?

📖 Do people still love "the wages of *unrighteousness*" today? What are some examples of this facing the church in the modern era?

Notes:

WORD

Remember back to Peter's purpose statements in 1:12-15 and 3:1-2. His desire is to remind his readers of the things of God that they already know. In 3:2, Peter cautions them to "remember the *words* spoken beforehand by the holy prophets and the commandment of the Lord and Savior *spoken* by your apostles." These Christians have no legitimate excuse if they are seduced away from the faith with false *words*. God has communicated to them in no uncertain terms. Whether they are Jews or Gentiles, they have the *knowledge* of God that they need to stay faithful. Notice that Peter reminds them that they have God's *Word* made sure through Jesus, His apostles, the prophets of old, preachers (e.g. Noah – 2:5), and even have letters from the apostle Paul! (cf. 3:14-16)

WORD	GREEK-R	TRANSLITERATION	OCCURRENCES	SUGGESTED SYMBOL
Word	λεγω	*legō*	8	~~Word~~

~~choosing~~   ~~unreasoning~~

Marked: ☐   **My Mark:**

2 Pet. 1:10	certain about His calling and	choosing	you; for as long as you practice
2 Pet. 1:19	*So* we have the prophetic	word	*made* more sure, to which you do
2 Pet. 2:3	they will exploit you with false	words	; their judgment from long ago is
2 Pet. 2:12	But these, like	unreasoning	animals, born as creatures of
2 Pet. 3:2	should remember the words	spoken	beforehand by the holy prophets
2 Pet. 3:4	and	saying	, "Where is the promise of His
2 Pet. 3:5	escapes their notice that by the	word	of God *the* heavens existed long
2 Pet. 3:7	But by His	word	the present heavens and earth are

WORD	GREEK-R	TRANSLITERATION	OCCURRENCES	SUGGESTED SYMBOL
Scripture	γραφω	*graphō*	4	Scripture

Marked: ☐   **My Mark:**

2 Pet. 1:20	first of all, that no prophecy of	Scripture	is *a matter* of one's own

2 Pet. 3:1	beloved, the second letter I am	writing	to you in which I am stirring up
2 Pet. 3:15	to the wisdom given him,	wrote	to you,
2 Pet. 3:16	as *they do* also the rest of the	Scriptures	, to their own destruction.

WORD	GREEK-R	TRANSLITERATION	OCCURRENCES	SUGGESTED SYMBOL
Speak	λαλεω	*laleō*	2	◁Speak◁

Marked: ☐   My Mark:

2 Pet. 1:21	but men moved by the Holy Spirit	spoke	from God.
2 Pet. 3:16	as also in all *his* letters,	speaking	in them of these things, in which

WORD	GREEK-R	TRANSLITERATION	OCCURRENCES	SUGGESTED SYMBOL
Called	καλεω	*kaleō*	2	◁Called◁

Marked: ☐   My Mark:

2 Pet. 1:3	the true knowledge of Him who	called	us by His own glory and
2 Pet. 1:10	to make certain about His	calling	and choosing you; for as long as

Study:

- Mark the term *words* (*rēma*) in 3:2 as another "speaking term" in 2 Peter with a similar symbol as *legō*.

    Marked: ☐   My Mark:

- You may also want to mark the translator's (NASB) inserted term "words" in 2 Peter 2:18 with a similar symbol as *legō*.

    Marked: ☐   My Mark:

- Peter's second letter showcases a "war of words" – The Word of Almighty God versus the false words of the false teachers. God's Word is holy and characterized by righteousness. The false teachers' words are flattering and empty. Make lists of the terms used to describe each side's words. For instance, God's Word is like a lamp shining in a dark place (1:19), spoken through true prophets and apostles (3:2), etc. Comparatively the false teachers' words are destructive (2:1), arrogant (2:18), mocking (3:3), etc.

God's Word:

Words of False Teachers:

Question:

- Peter says in 2:3 that the false teachers "in *their* greed will exploit you with false *words*." How do you suppose these Christians were being exploited with false *words*? What are some ways in which people try to exploit Christians with false *words* today?

- What are some things Peter mentions that the *Word* of God accomplishes in the natural universe? (e.g. 3:5-7; 10-11)

📖 According to Peter, what are some things that the *Word* of God does for the Christian?

Notes:

JUDGMENT

The concept of God's *judgment* in the Scriptures does not always necessarily mean an unfavorable outcome. God has told us elsewhere in His Word (e.g. 2 Corinthians 5:10; John 5:28-29; etc.) that everyone will be *judged* accordingly and that the *righteous* will be with Him eternally. The false teachers and unprincipled men Peter writes about will be *judged* accordingly, and it's not looking good. As it stands at the time Peter writes of these men, they are being *kept/reserved* for punishment. That's not to say that they can't repent before the *Day* of *Judgment*, but their heinous deeds and selfish ambitions at the expense of God's people remove all doubt in Peter's mind concerning their *judgment*, which is not idle, and their *destruction*, which is not asleep (2 Peter 2:3; cf. Jude 4).

WORD	GREEK-R	TRANSLITERATION	OCCURRENCES	SUGGESTED SYMBOL
Judgment	κρινω	*krinō*	7	Judgment

Marked: ☐   **My Mark:**

2 Pet. 2:3	you with false words; their	judgment	from long ago is not idle, and
2 Pet. 2:4	to pits of darkness, reserved for	judgment	;
2 Pet. 2:6	and *if* He	condemned	the cities of Sodom and Gomorrah
2 Pet. 2:9	under punishment for the day of	judgment	,
2 Pet. 2:11	and power do not bring a reviling	judgment	against them before the Lord.
2 Pet. 3:1	in which I am stirring up your	sincere	mind by way of reminder,
2 Pet. 3:7	for fire, kept for the day of	judgment	and destruction of ungodly men.

WORD	GREEK-R	TRANSLITERATION	OCCURRENCES	SUGGESTED SYMBOL
Kept	τηρεω	*tēreō*	4	(Kept)

Marked: ☐   **My Mark:**

2 Pet. 2:4	them to pits of darkness,	reserved	for judgment;
2 Pet. 2:9	the godly from temptation, and to	keep	the unrighteous under punishment
2 Pet. 2:17	the black darkness has been	reserved	.
2 Pet. 3:7	are being reserved for fire,	kept	for the day of judgment and

Study:

🔍 Mark the term *reserved* (*thēsaurizō*) in 3:7 with the same symbol as *tēreō* since it is contextually synonymous.

Marked: ☐ | **My Mark:** |

Question:

📖 Peter gives several examples of those who received an unfavorable *judgment* and experienced condemnation for turning away from God, but his preferred illustration is that of the global flood in Genesis. He mentions the flood in 1 Peter 3:19-21, 2 Peter 2:5, and 2 Peter 3:5-6. Why do you think Peter revisits this instance of *judgment* more than that of Sodom and Gomorrah, rebellious angels, Balaam, etc.?

📖 What major reasons does Peter give to demonstrate that God's *judgment* of the flood on the world was just? (cf. 2 Peter 2:5)

📖 Genesis 18:16-33 is the account of Abraham deliberating with God regarding the *judgment* of Sodom and Gomorrah. Read this account and compare it with Peter's words in 2 Peter 2:6-9. What key word do these accounts share? What does it seem God is concerned with when passing *judgment*? (cf. 2 Corinthians 5:21)

Notes:

GODLINESS

Again, *godliness* and *righteousness* stand as major contrasts to their counterparts of *ungodly* and *unrighteousness* in this letter. There are clear standards of lifestyle and conduct that matter to God. And God tells us that we can know exactly how to live *godly* lives and avoid the past mistakes of others who sought their own *ungodly* ambitions. "Seeing that His divine power has granted to us everything pertaining to life and *godliness*, through the true *knowledge* of Him who called us by His own glory and excellence" (2 Peter 1:3).

WORD	GREEK-L	TRANSLITERATION	OCCURRENCES	SUGGESTED SYMBOL
Godliness	εὐσέβεια	*eusebeia*	4	Godliness

Marked: ☐ **My Mark:**

2 Pet. 1:3	everything pertaining to life and	godliness	, through the true knowledge of
2 Pet. 1:6	and in *your* perseverance,	godliness	,
2 Pet. 1:7	and in *your*	godliness	, brotherly kindness, and in *your*
2 Pet. 3:11	you to be in holy conduct and	godliness	,

WORD	GREEK-L	TRANSLITERATION	OCCURRENCES	SUGGESTED SYMBOL
Godly	εὐσεβής	*eusebēs*	1	Godly

Marked: ☐ **My Mark:**

2 Pet. 2:9	knows how to rescue the	godly	from temptation, and to keep the

WORD	GREEK-L	TRANSLITERATION	OCCURRENCES	SUGGESTED SYMBOL
Ungodly	ἀσεβής	asebēs	3	Ungodly

Marked: ☐   **My Mark:**

2 Pet. 2:5	a flood upon the world of the	ungodly	;
2 Pet. 2:6	example to those who would live	ungodly	lives thereafter;
2 Pet. 3:7	of judgment and destruction of	ungodly	men.

Study:

🔍 Define *godliness* (*eusebeia*) and *ungodly* (*asebēs*) using your Bible dictionary. What other helpful or interesting aspects are seen in their definitions?

Definition of *godliness* (*eusebeia*):

Definition of *ungodly* (*asebēs*):

🔍 Peter uses the word for *ungodly* once in his first letter. If you'd like, mark the reference to *godless* (*asebēs*) in 1 Peter 4:18 with the same symbol as *ungodly*.

Marked: ☐   **My Mark:**

🔍 Just as you made a list of synonyms to *ungodly* and *unrighteous* under the section for *Righteous*, now make another list of terms that coincide with *godliness* and *righteousness*.

Examples: *moral excellence* (1:5; cf. 1:5-7) – *holy conduct* (3:11) – *spotless/ blameless* (3:14) – etc.

Marked: ☐   **My Mark:**

Synonyms to godliness and righteousness:

Question:

- Peter is very encouraging when he says in 2:9 that "the Lord knows how to rescue the *godly* from temptation." Verses 5 and 7 of the same chapter tell us that God "preserved Noah" and that "He rescued righteous Lot." Did God just snap His fingers and snatch these men out of their circumstances? How did He deliver them? What are some general principles we need to keep in mind when needing God's rescue?

- Regarding the destruction of Sodom and Gomorrah, Peter states that God "made them an example to those who would live *ungodly* lives thereafter" (2 Peter 2:6; cf. Jude 7). Although these broken circumstances are horrible, God used them for the benefit of others. What are some other seemingly bad things that God has used (or **can** use) for the benefit of future generations?

Notes:

WAY

The concept of the right *way* versus the wrong *way* is a familiar one in the New Testament. For instance, Jesus speaks of the broad *way* that leads to destruction and the narrow *way* that leads to life (Matthew 7:13-14). The word itself is translated as *road, journey, path, street, travel,* etc. At the spiritual level, it ultimately comes down to choice. Each individual has freewill to choose the path he or she will *follow* – how he will act, who she'll spend her time with, what he'll listen to. *Follow* and *own* are included in this section as "Optional Words" since they are contextually related to *way* in the case of individual choice and personal responsibility. Peter assures these Christians that the false teachers are the only ones to blame for their "*own* destruction" (3:16) and that they themselves need to be careful not to fall from their "*own* steadfastness" (3:17).

WORD	GREEK-R	TRANSLITERATION	OCCURRENCES	SUGGESTED SYMBOL
Way	οδος	*odos*	6	

Marked: ☐   **My Mark:**

2 Pet. 1:11	for in this way the	entrance	into the eternal kingdom of our
2 Pet. 1:15	that at any time after my	departure	you will be able to call these
2 Pet. 2:2	and because of them the	way	of the truth will be maligned;
2 Pet. 2:15	forsaking the right	way	, they have gone astray, having
2 Pet. 2:15	gone astray, having followed the	way	of Balaam, the *son* of Beor, who
2 Pet. 2:21	for them not to have known the	way	of righteousness, than having

Study:

🔍 If you'd like, mark the references to *own* (*idios*) and *follow* (*akoloutheō*). (See "Optional Words" for symbol suggestions.)

Own (*idios*): 1:3, 20; 2:16, 22; 3:3, 16, 17

Marked: ☐   **My Mark:**

Follow (*akoloutheō*): 1:16; 2:2, 15

Marked: ☐   **My Mark:**

Question:

📖 *Follow* (*akoulutheō*) is used three times in 2 Peter. What things does Peter caution God's people not to *follow*?

📖 As a fisherman, Peter understands the concept of bait. And it's not just for fish. He says that the false teachers are skilled in the art of *enticing* (2 Peter 2:14, 18). What methods were they using to *entice* God's people? Does this still happen today? What are some examples?

📖 If a Christian wanders away from "the way of the truth," who is ultimately responsible? Why? (cf. 3:17; Acts 13:8-10)

📖 Are you *following* the right *way*? According to Peter, how do you know? (cf. 1 Peter 2:21)

Notes:

PROMISE

One does not have to read too far into the Bible to find that God is a God of amazing *promises*. Big *promises*. Kept *promises*. Whether or not the men of old who received God's *promises* (e.g. Noah, Abraham, David, etc.) understood every nuance to the guarantees, it was always certain that God delivered what was pledged in perfect time and fashion. Peter illuminates this quality of God by reminding his readers that He never let anyone down and isn't about to start now. Mockers may question God's *promises* (3:3-9), but they're the ones who have the imperfect track record. With their flattering speech, the false teachers make empty *promises* of freedom, something they cannot deliver since they themselves are "slaves of corruption" (2:19). The Lord delivers. Fast talkers do not.

WORD	GREEK-R	TRANSLITERATION	OCCURRENCES	SUGGESTED SYMBOL
Promise	επαγγελια	*epangelia*	5	Promise

Marked: ☐

My Mark:

2 Pet. 1:4	us His precious and magnificent	promises	, so that by them you may become
2 Pet. 2:19		promising	them freedom while they themselves
2 Pet. 3:4	and saying, "Where is the	promise	of His coming? For *ever* since the
2 Pet. 3:9	The Lord is not slow about His	promise	, as some count slowness, but is
2 Pet. 3:13	But according to His	promise	we are looking for new heavens and

Question:

📖 God's "magnificent *promises*" in 1:4 are not specifically identified. Given Peter's knowledge of the Old Testament, his intimate relationship with Jesus while He walked the earth, and the context of the passage, what do you think these *promises* of God might be referring to?

📖 What were the false teachers promising these Christians in 2:19? What is ironic about their *promises*? (cf. Romans 6:6; John 8:34)

📖 What *promises* of God does Peter assure his readers will come to pass?

📖 What *promises* of God do you most look forward to seeing take shape in your own life?

Notes:

OPTIONAL WORDS

WORD	TRANSLITERATION	OCC...	SUGGESTED SYMBOL	MARKED
Lord	*kyrios*	14	▽ Lord	☐
Jesus	*Iēsous*	9	Jesus ✝	☐
Christ	*Christos*	8	Christ	☐
God	*theos*	7	△ God	☐
Own	*idios*	7	⬭ Own	☐
Follow	*akoloutheō*	3	Follow	☐
Truth	*alētheia*	3	Truth	☐
Right	*euthus*	1	Right	☐

My Mark:	My Mark:
My Mark:	My Mark:
My Mark:	My Mark:
My Mark:	My Mark:

Notes:

KEY CONCLUSIONS

THEME OF 2 PETER:

MAJOR TOPICS IN 2 PETER:

APPLICATIONS FROM 2 PETER:

MY KEY WORDS

WORD	CHAPTER(S)	OCCURRENCES	SYMBOL	MARKED
				☐
				☐
				☐
				☐
				☐
				☐
				☐
				☐
				☐
				☐
				☐
				☐
				☐
				☐
				☐

www.ingramcontent.com/pod-product-compliance
Lightning Source LLC
Chambersburg PA
CBHW042015120526
44592CB00043B/2870